*Search Engines
Handbook*

Search Engines Handbook

by NED L. FIELDEN *and*
LUCY KUNTZ

McFarland & Company, Inc., Publishers
Jefferson, North Carolina, and London

To my father, Lee Fielden,
who steadfastly held that it was
always possible to learn something new.

Library of Congress Cataloguing-in-Publication Data

Fielden, Ned L.
    Search engines handbook / by Ned L. Fielden and Lucy Kuntz.
        p.   cm.
    Includes bibliographical references and index.
    ISBN 0-7864-1308-5 (softcover : 60# alkaline paper) ∞
    1. Search engines—Handbooks, manuals, etc.   I. Kuntz, Lucy,
    1967–   II. Title.
    TK5105.884.F54   2002
    025.04 — dc21   2001007409

British Library cataloguing data are available

Front cover image: ©2002 Digital Vision

Manufactured in the United States of America

McFarland & Company, Inc., Publishers
    Box 611, Jefferson, North Carolina 28640
        www.mcfarlandpub.com

Acknowledgments

As is always the case with any human endeavor, this book had lots of help in its creation. Our interest in Information Retrieval and the nasty details of searching mechanisms began many years ago, with the prodding of professors Bill Cooper and Ray Larson of the University of California Berkeley Library School, now the School of Information Management and Systems.

Colleagues at San Francisco State University have helped with numerous ideas: thanks go to Gina Castro, Christy Graham, Caroline Harnly, Nina Hagiwara, Robin Imhof, Tom Iwatsubo, LaVonne Jacobsen, Chris Mays, and Jeff Rosen.

Lorca Hanns, webmaster for the SFSU bookstore, has been generous with his knowledge and astute in his suggestions.

Members of the SFSU library's Document Delivery Services Kathleen Messer, Nathan Conkle and Shawn Heiser indulged us with frequent and unpredictable use of their fax machine.

Contents

Preface

This book is aimed at a wide spectrum of readers. It should be a functional introductory guide for anyone from high school students on up. Our own professional focus is on higher education — college and university level research — but we have tried to keep our focus wide, and hope this work is suitable for anyone who uses the Internet to find information.

For anyone engaged in instruction involving Internet search engines and directories, this book could certainly be helpful, either as a text or as a background contribution to pedagogical thought. We have been using Internet protocols for over ten years now, have run classes and workshops for a wide range of people, and have experience with Information Retrieval principles. A great many people have an interest in becoming adept at the use of Internet searching tools, and there are strong reasons to hope that a critical mass of searchers can develop who both understand good Internet searching mechanisms and some of the issues surrounding information and its use in contemporary society. We hope to reach most of this group.

This book is organized into six chapters. The Introduction (Chapter 1) sets the stage and gives the reader some idea of where the book will take them, while Chapter 2 is a non-technical discussion of the operation and construction of search engines. This is necessarily an oversimplified narrative, since the details of search engine design are often proprietary and closely guarded secrets. The vast complexities of operations done behind the great screen of Oz also strongly urge a simplified explanation on our part. The mathematics and conceptual framework are all the purview of very smart, very well trained people. While not designers ourselves, we have a very healthy respect for the work that gets done in search engine design.

Chapter 3 is the practical chapter and outlines the basics of good Internet search strategy. Our experience over the years in various Internet and online searching arenas, we hope, has provided us with a good basis for advice, a sense of context, and a sound framework for searchers more newly arrived to the online neighborhood.

Chapter 4 takes the measure of a good handful of search engines, while Chapter 5 does the same for a smaller handful of important directories. We have not been comprehensive, but selective in our lists, and the various search engines and directories mentioned here are either especially valuable or important in some way.

Chapter 6 is speculative, and outlines some potential directions that Internet search engine design may follow. A glossary and bibliography round out the work.

Several assumptions are made: We expect that the reader has had some experience, however fleeting, with the Internet. Perhaps a visit to a portal like Yahoo!, AOL, or MSN. The reader should know something about how a browser works, how the Graphical User Interface that involves a mouse and a point-and-click approach to Internet navigation gets one from here to there.

Familiarity with browser functions like bookmarks would be helpful, so that one can save favorite destinations for future reference. If one is serious about developing skills, one might even want to bookmark *this* book's "page," which has every URL mentioned in the work, as well as some supplemental material. This page is at http://www.library.sfsu.edu/fielden/seh.htm. The tendency for Internet addresses to disappear or migrate elsewhere necessitates this approach if the information listed is to stay current, accurate and usable.

When a term that is to be found in the glossary is mentioned for the first time in the text, it appears in bold. We have avoided excessive technical jargon, but the appearance of several unfamiliar terms should not be discouraging. There is considerable change potential for the World Wide Web with respect to information retrieval possibilities, and it would not hurt to have more people understand some of the issues that surround this dynamic arena.

While every attempt has been made to provide current information, two changes have occurred for sites mentioned in this work since manuscript preparation — a URL change for Excite (along with some other revisions) and Northern Light's decision to no longer remain a free site. The book's webpage will maintain current information.

N.L.F. & L.K.
Berkeley, California
February 2002

1

Introduction

*Any sufficiently advanced technology
is indistinguishable from magic.* —Arthur C. Clarke.

By the turn of the 21st century, the Internet had become a favored place to seek information. When people went looking for answers to questions, they increasingly turned to the Internet. Certain topical arenas have been particularly well served by an Internet characterized by rapid speed and easy access: travel and jobs, certain business data sets (up-to-date currency exchange rates, stock prices, etc.), news (newspapers invariably have an online presence), sports and entertainment.

This trend is hardly surprising, given the growth of the Internet made possible by the development in the early and mid–1990's of World Wide Web browsers like Netscape's Navigator and Microsoft's Internet Explorer, and the emergence of the Internet as a global network, no longer limited merely to research functions practiced at universities and government agencies.

What is surprising, and occasionally troubling, is the tendency for people to look to the Internet first for information that they traditionally would have found in printed format at a library or elsewhere in books: demographic data, history, literary reviews, and medical information, for a beginning list. Finding quality information for whatever purpose is a goal of many people, and the Internet has become a staging ground for research of all varieties.

A Nielsen/NetRatings estimate of Internet size in August 2001*

*http://pm.netratings.com/nnpm/owa/NRpublicreports.toppropertiesweekly [August, 2001].

lists the top twenty-five visited sites on the Internet. The first is media godzilla AOL Time Warner, followed by many other media goliaths (MSN, Walt Disney, AT&T) but throughout the mix are a fair number of sites whose primary focus is getting users to their information destinations: Yahoo!, Excite, Google, iWon, Ask Jeeves, and GoTo. Clearly Internet searching tools are important and popular.

That as a group humans are a curious lot would not surprise anyone from Aristotle to Bill Gates. That humans use the most readily available and easiest medium to find whatever it is they seek is no news to anyone who has studied hunter/gatherer societies or the economics of information.

Yet this business of looking to the Internet for answers to all and every question is nonetheless remarkable from both a historical and a practical standpoint.

We will not examine why this has happened, although we may marvel at the results from a safe distance. Instead we want to look at the Internet finding apparatus, the Internet **search engines** and **directories** that are the focus of this book. The manner in which they are designed, constructed, and operate alters our lives, and has helped change the basic ways that modern humans look for information. For us all to use them wisely means we need to know more about how they work and what they include.

What you want out of a search engine and what you get are often two different things. Why is this? Why cannot computer-assisted tools just pluck the information needed out of the ethersphere and deliver it to you in readily digestible, clearly understandable format? Surely the best minds of the computer and information management world are at work on this vexing issue, so why are not results better?

With the intrusion of computers into contemporary life at the turn of the millennium, after a siege of scarcely 15 years (for personal computers), it is not always easy to remember that they are human creations. They are not mind-readers, any more than your psychotherapists or gardeners are, but many people attribute impossible qualities to their operation. We hope to examine some of the strengths and weaknesses of search engines during the course of this work, and to do this we need to look behind the scenes a bit.

We have never felt the calling to become search engine designers ourselves (although through our training we have perhaps come closer to this fate than much of the rest of the populace) and instead are just users, people who like good tools for finding what we need. Our perspective is that of advocates for those who use search engines.

Our interests pose a number of questions: Why are search engines hard to use? How much does a lousy **interface** interfere with good results? How much can commercial pressures pollute the ability to locate quality information sources?

Hunter-Gatherers on the Internet

Finding things is an ancient art well built into our conscious functions. Despite its long tradition in our species' history, it remains an elusive topic of study.

How do we, as humans, go about deciding what we want and then trying to locate it? The answers are easier when the sought item is concrete (a job, an apartment to rent, a lover) and much more difficult when entering the realm of more amorphous interests. When looking for answers to questions, how does one know where to begin or what to look for?

Research methods are generally a poorly understood area, and one that is often marginally taught even at elite universities. Very often it is not until graduate study that students are given thorough, explicit advice about research methods.

Individual teachers in high school and professors at undergraduate levels often provide good models and pose worthy research challenges, but these efforts are generally isolated and not part of a broader spectrum of a movement which has come to be called **Information Literacy**. This concept is defined variously, but essentially means a person's ability to develop questions about a topic, find information on that topic, and intelligently apply the information thus found.

Before the Internet and the widespread availability of online databases in the last ten years, college level research was both easier to understand and more pedestrian. Journal articles, which form the backbone of a large majority of upper level research, particularly in the sciences, were the sources deemed most worthy of study for any given topic.

While there were plenty of **indexes** to use to locate articles on a given subject, these were virtually all print resources (hardcopy) and resided in university libraries. Their utility was assured by a rigorous review process, peer review, which served to keep the quality of the information very high, as any article that was published had to receive the review and approval of specialists in that field. The reach of the Internet and online databases has changed much of this.

Not all information gathering should take place on the Internet. Huge areas and topics are still best studied by resorting to time-honored resources — books and journal articles written by professionals. But professionals were also some of the earliest people to begin to take advantage of the speed and range of scholarly communication possible with the Internet.

LOCATION APPROACHES

How do you know what you want if you cannot find even the words to describe what it is you seek? Desired information and words are inextricably linked, and generating the words for your desire is often the first and perhaps most important task. This is especially true on the Internet, which despite the increasing saturation of images and other non-text formats, remains a word-based environment.

There are two basic approaches to finding information on the Internet. There is the "human assisted" approach, with Internet indexes and directories as examples, and the "computer assisted" approach, with search engines as the main example.

Neither of these external mechanisms can entirely replace the best asset of all, your own native cunning. Your own inquisitive nature and your instincts for judging good information, combined with continual education and a sound critical faculty, are your best bets for superior results.

The capacity to think clearly about an issue, to frame the problem and pose questions that can be answered, is one of the hallmarks of good research everywhere. Good questions can lead to good answers. Conventional wisdom holds that "there is no such thing as a stupid question," but certainly people can pose some questions that are more thoughtless than others.

The successful researchers that you know are likely to have the same set of qualities: an ability to focus on the task at hand, a creative approach to problem solving, and an ability to "fail well." The first two are obvious in their meaning, but the second requires further thought.

Failure is a common element of most human endeavor. Moon landings and DNA decipherment could not be possible without making some fairly major mistakes. Failure is a great, perhaps the paramount, teacher. In our personal lives, failure haunts us relentlessly in small and large ways, and the fear of failure drives a great many human activities.

"Failing well" as an online researcher means learning from searches that didn't work on the first try. It is an optimistic stance, a recognition that one can learn from all kinds of situations. Even the best searchers we know fail a lot of times in their searches, but they have a willingness and ability to rethink their topic and reformulate their search in a way that leads them to their desired goal.

Internet searching apparatus should be like good tools everywhere: they should be easy to use and apply, produce consistent (or at least satisfactory) results, and "feel" right while in use. Our position is that it helps to know how one's tools are made to help understand how to use them, and what they are capable of doing.

SEARCH ENGINE DESIGN

Search engines need to be designed, constructed, and maintained by several different types of people. Obviously the computer science people are primary: those who make the processors, arrange database structure and design the overall architecture of computer operation.

The network people need good computers to work with and the capacity to allow traffic to the search engine to be handled with speed and ease. Applied mathematics makes a big difference for the indexing and finding mechanisms of a search engine. The conceptual framework of the field of **Information Retrieval** has contributed mightily to the development of the search engines, with a great deal of the theoretical work done quite some time ago.

The size and Byzantine nature of the Web itself has complicated life, and some creative solutions have been found and continue to be sought to penetrate its peculiarities. Designers who make the interface, which after all is what the users see and utilize for their needs, have their work cut out for them, for a good interface is dazzlingly difficult to make. With luck, designers are familiar with the principles of the field of **Human Computer Interaction**, which examines how man and machine meet and mate. Using this expertise, they can construct interfaces that are easy to use and not confusing.

The results of a search similarly should be displayed clearly and in a manner that is both useful (with solid, current links to document locations) and in a mode that facilitates the searcher's ability to run another search, perhaps a modified or clarified version of the initial search.

We will look at the way search engines are put together, how they run, how they locate information and display it for your use. We will also toss out some practical suggestions gained from many years of using Internet searching tools, and try to provide a sound platform from which to engage your own efforts. One goal is to include enough theoretical information to provide a framework for understanding, without overloading the non-specialist with a surfeit of detail.

Selected search engines and directories are listed and discussed as examples of the state of the Web at the moment — this list will likely alter over time as extinctions and mutations occur. This year's David is likely to be next year's Goliath, and then perhaps extinct (or perhaps worse, bought and neglected) a short time later.

We will put all **URLs** listed in the book on a webpage for your reference [http://www. library.sfsu.edu/fielden/seh.htm], so that we can update them over time, given the tendency for Internet addresses to die off or migrate suddenly.

Comparisons between the Internet and frontier life were common in the days just before the Internet's truly explosive growth in the early 1990's. It was regarded as a strange new land, and its promise and resources seemed limitless. Now it has jostled its way into mainstream society, and an inversion has occurred — in many communities it has become harder to find someone without an email address than someone who does have one.

The directories and search engines put together by a variety of Internet community members, from both the private and public sector, have been an exciting development in the search for information. We will leave it to you to decide whether they have evolved sufficiently to be considered magical.

2
How Search Engines Work

We have become a people unable to comprehend the technology we invent.—Association of American Colleges Report, 1985.

How DOES a search engine work, anyway?

The short answer is that search engines are nothing more than automated software that matches a searcher's topic terms (**keywords**) with an indexed list of documents found on the Web or in some other collection, arranges that list according to some order of relevancy, and provides **hyperlinks** to those documents so that they may be visited.

The history and development of search engines is an interesting story all by itself, but their main functions remain disarmingly simple.

WORD MATCHING

It turns out that one of the activities at which computers excel is finding and matching terms. This feature has been utilized by the computer community for a very long time — the speed and accuracy of text term recognition by a computer far surpasses human capabilities. A document several hundred pages long can be scanned for a particular term and the list of its occurrences in that document can be prepared in a blazingly short amount of time, by even fairly pedestrian desktop computers.

This mechanism is applied in such popular features as the spell-check function found on word processing programs like Word or Wordperfect. When summoned, the spellchecker application scans an entire document's compilation of words, word by word, and highlights words that do not match its list of acceptable (usually derived from a dictionary of some sort or another) terms. The user is given some choices to select alternative (standardized) spellings, and the whole business has become so quick and easy that now one rarely even gives it a thought, except when something goes amiss.

The word-matching capacity of computers is central to the development of search engines. It is the facet most obvious to anyone who has ever typed in a set of search terms into a search engine's query window.

This word-matching faculty is such an immediate part of the search engine operation that it is tempting to downplay what else is going on behind the scenes. We will now take a look at search engine infrastructure and functionality.

LOCATING DOCUMENTS

Before its highly developed computer search **algorithms** can do anything, a search engine must have a collection of documents to look through. Currently Internet search engines vary greatly in the size of their collections, which can range from Excite's still impressive 250 million Web pages to estimates of well over half a billion pages for several others.

How did these search engines get such huge collections, which dwarf even the book collections of very large research libraries like Harvard (14 million books and documents*) or the University of California's entire library system?

The search engine collections are built by means of automated programs called a variety of names; **bots, spiders,** and **crawlers** are common designations. These "crawler" programs are set loose to

*http://vpf-Web.harvard.edu/factbook/00-01/page31.htm [Sept. 2001].

"Go ask your search engine."

comb the Internet for documents, and they are set up to prepare lists of lists with document information (information about information.) Our explanation of their operation is oversimplified, but gives a rough idea of how they work.

Crawlers are not actually literally set loose to hunt through websites, although this is what they functionally do. They are a program that resides on a computer (a "**client**") which then sends out requests for information to a Web address at another computer (a "**server**").

This relationship between client and server (and exchange of information) is the basis for what the Web is all about — the crawlers use the same standard method of making requests and "visiting" websites as you do at your own Web browser, although due to their automated nature they take advantage of some shortcuts and speed.

Jeff Prosise once described a crawler program thusly: "A Web robot is a browser with an autopilot."*

Crawlers can find only documents already targeted by hyperlinks that reside on pages they already know about. Hyperlinks, or links for short, are one of the primary facets of the World Wide Web, and allow you to move quickly and easily from place to place around the Web.

The crawlers must begin with a starter page, and then they follow the hyperlinks of that page to other pages, then take those links and follow them further.

In other words, it is like finding out about other people by asking only those who have direct communication with them. Person A knows person B, C and D well enough to have direct contact. By talking to persons, B,C, and D, you discover they know persons E, F, G and H, and the list grows quickly.

Instructions are given to the crawlers regarding what to look for and what to grab. At minimum, the crawlers take a document's (website's) title and URL, sometimes more information. A list is created with the linked bits of information.

Often the whole process is a multi-stage affair, where a first pass will garner a list which is then "crawled" again by another crawler program (sometimes called a "harvester" for its more specialized retrieval mechanisms) to expand the amount of information attached to a given document.

The instructions given these crawlers regarding the amount and kind of information they retrieve determines the "depth" and "breadth" of indexing. Many decisions have to be made in the design phase about what exactly they should do, and trade-offs in performance are unavoidable.

*PC Magazine, v. 15, no. 13, 5 July 1996.

Crawler Introductions

A crawler cannot begin its work without a starting point. It must have a known page, a website with hyperlinks to follow. It is like sending some friends into a room of crowded people attending a conference. Each friend needs an introduction (a hyperlink) in order to meet other people there. A friend can begin with one person, who if he/she knows anyone else in the room, can then move to them, find out who they know and make their way around the room. When your friend gets to someone with no other friends (no other links) there is nowhere to go but back. Your friend returns to the person who sent them on to the one friendless person, a virtual orphan, and follows another second introduction to someone else, hopefully with knowledge of others. In this way the crawlers/friends make their way about. The instructions given your friend determine whether to go for breadth or depth. In the first case, the friend may frenetically bounce around the room, following introductions to a wide array of other people, and then come back to follow secondary introductions. In the second case the friend is a party parasite, who when meeting a new person plies them with questions and follows every single introduction, only to come back immediately to follow another. The first system will generate a broad network of connections quickly, the second will be thorough but slower, and get to know the room full of people more completely, at the price of speed of coverage.

The "depth-first" crawlers will explore a page from top to bottom and save linked URLs for further study. The "breadth-first" crawlers do not do top-to-bottom pages but rather cast a wide net, following links to many different servers before coming back to the original starting place. The "depth-first" crawlers will run through a whole site first, before exploring linkages elsewhere.

There are also differences in the amount of information gathered, dependent on the instructions given the crawler.

Some search engines just grab a title and perhaps the first paragraph (or first 50 words) of the document. Others scan the entire text of the document to create a "full-text" index, including all the hyperlinks, and the **metadata** (information on information, more on this in a moment). The purpose is to build an index of keywords from the document, that can then be put to use in a larger index. Obviously, even for fast, automated bots, the less information collected, the faster the process of indexing can take place.

The size of the Web makes the whole process of indexing an extremely daunting task. If you think about what it would take to make a database or catalog of all the books (or CDs, or movie videos) that you own, and then think about what you would have to do to do this for every other single person's collection around the world, you get an idea of the magnitude of the issues involved.

In general, one of the main problems with search engines is not that they will not find a Web document that matches a user's request,

---

Size of the Web

One thing that makes a difference among search engines is the overall size of the index and how comprehensively the index covers the Web. Estimates of the World Wide Web's size begin at over a billion pages and go on from there. These are estimates of publicly available sectors of the Web, not its totality. This is the arena that crawlers can reach. The non-public area has come to be called the "**invisible Web**" or the "unseen Web." This idea is not unlike the "dark matter" of the universe that cosmologists and physicists contemplate, the material of the universe that cannot be accounted for by counting stars and calculating the mass of the obvious other material of the universe. This unseen Web is a significant portion of the Web since it includes sectors like corporate Intranets, information structures available only to the company itself or its clients, as well as large databases of information only available by subscription. It also includes any page that requires data entry, such as filling out a form or a purchase order, or a page that asks that crawlers not visit them (which could be a request made for a variety of reasons and is known as a "robot exclusion" command, a text field in the page's description). The Web's size is staggering, whether publicly available or not, but one should remember that no Internet search ever encompasses the totality of the beast.

but that they find such an overwhelming flood of documents that it is hard to separate out the most useful ones.

METADATA

The search engines usually collect some information on the kind of document found — whether it is a text document, a video, a music file or whatever. Additional information is often included in the document's fields called **metatags**. These can be: author name, description of the document (usually a short one sentence summary of the document) and "keywords," or descriptive words that provide some clue as to the document's nature and characteristics.

All of this is done "behind the scenes"— it is not apparent to you when you visit a website whether this information is present or not. Some search engines pay attention to it, others ignore it. For an example of what this metadata looks like, these are the metadata fields displayed for the illustration of the search engine comparison chart pictured on page 32. (You can view these hidden tags yourself by using the browser's "View" menu to pick "Page source" or "Source").

```
<!— METADATA using the Dublin Core —>
 <LINK REL = SCHEMA.dc HREF="http://purl.org/metadata/
dublin_ core">
 <META NAME="DC.title" CONTENT="Search Tools Chart">
 <META NAME="DC.creator" CONTENT="Carole Leita">
 <META NAME="DC.publisher" CONTENT="InFoPeople Project,
California State Library">
 <META NAME="DC.description" CONTENT="A quick guide
(cheat-sheet) to Internet search engines and subject directories.">
 <META NAME="DC.identifier" CONTENT="http://www.info
people.org/">
 <META NAME="DC.subject" CONTENT="search tools, searching
help, research chart, search chart, finding aid, finding information
guide, search guide, cheatsheet, cheat-sheet">
```

The metadata for this page is more organized than for most webpages, as it conforms to the Dublin Core, a set of standards developed for Web documents. Included you can see the document's

author name listed under "creator," as well as description and subject (which are standardized terms, and you may notice other pages
do not have this standardized vocabulary but may just list "meta keywords" in this field).

How the data is arranged in a text file shapes to some extent
how the retrieval of the records will proceed later. Heroic attempts
are made to make the structure of index tables simple and short, so
that retrieval does not take too much time.

DOCUMENT INDEXING

Why make an index?

Information that is unorganized can prove impossible to search,
as the owner of any attic well knows. An index is an attempt to impose
some sort of logical order on a pile of items, and is often done by
having a name or number correspond to a paired location.

The index in this book lists a topic (Indexing) with a page location (this page, among others.) You can find your topic by looking
for it in the index list, and following its "pointer" location by page
number. Other types of indexes include items like a phone book
(linking names with telephone numbers) or library catalogs (books
or other materials with a call number or shelf location). Human
indexing is an art while automated indexing is a science, and the ten-
sion between these two approaches is an important one to consider
as we look at the various search engines and directories.

The Web indexes created by the various search engines are an
attempt to organize Internet information so that it can be found. Mathematical computations attempt to quantify relationships among documents and queries, so that document location is accurate and useful.

Some of the differences that one experiences while utilizing the
search engines can be explained by differences in the preparation of
the document index. Several factors come into play: index size (is bigger always better?), depth of indexing (how "much" of a document
is cataloged?) and breadth of indexing (what besides document title?
How many other hyperlinks are included?) and perhaps most

Spam, the Mosquitoes of the Internet

Spam avoidance is the single greatest difficulty posed to search engine designers. How do you get your search engine to avoid listing documents designed to deceive retrieval mechanisms? For the most part, spam is the perhaps inevitable result of commercial pressures. (There is a small but annoyingly dedicated percentage of folks who like to spam just for the thrill of it, but generally it is money that drives spam abuse). A website can make money, sometimes a lot of money, but generally only if it is visited. Web marketers talk about wanting "eyeballs"–visitors who view their site and the advertising often included there, and then follow those links to their sponsors. Companies selling everything from pornography to books and other services will often stop at nothing to find a way to get their site listed in the index of a search engine. There is a mad scramble for a visitor's attention, and getting someone to your site first before they discover a competitor's site becomes a single-minded focus for marketers. Since search engines are used so heavily by Web users to find information, high placement in a results list is an effective way to gain attention. Deceptive practices in the past have included false metadata description terms, large numbers of keywords that are invisible on the webpage but picked up by the crawlers (these could be text in tiny font, or text with the same color as the background of the page), or just an overabundance of the same keywords repeated over and over again. In the words of a designer from AltaVista "Spamming degrades the value of the index and is a nuisance for all."*

significantly, how well does the index avoid **spam**, or non-relevant "junk" material deliberately tossed into the mix by website creators hoping to lure visitors to their site?

Often it feels as if computers, with their unyielding binary approach, dividing the world into series of databits, either one or zero, nudge the rest of the universe in that direction as well.

In the arena of finding information utilizing the Internet, this division appears again — information is organized by humans (direc-

*http://help.altavista.com/adv_search/ast_haw_spam. [Sept. 2001].

tories and their brethren, virtual libraries) or by automated indexing mechanisms, which the search engines employ. This prompts some consideration of a given document's nature and content, and how we perceive it within our world of understanding.

Categories

What makes one item similar to another? How can we recognize similarities between groups of items? Humans use a variety of mechanisms to identify similar items. We have very evolved methods of identifying patterns, and can do so in a variety of ways. Some of our abilities show up in classification schemes, which attempt to order items into easily understood categories.

In making an index, one of the question that always arises is how to group things. Directories have a hierarchical structure created by humans. Is it possible the Web could arrange itself into categories? Would there be clustering of items, the same way that our universe seems to clump together stars and planets? Would it be possible to discern these patterns given enough computer power?

How can we determine a given document's degree of similarity with another? This is a vexing question, and leads us well beyond our main concern with search engines. If a particular book on lizards, for example, is found useful and instructive, perhaps there are other books that might be found with similar attributes that are also helpful.

Libraries for many many centuries have been in the business of finding ways to both group "like" things together, and provide a mechanism for finding specific items. United States libraries generally employ one of two possible classification schemes.

The first was developed by the founder of modern American Librarianship, Melvyl Dewey, and bears his name, the Dewey Decimal system. This is now utilized in American public and school libraries, as well as adopted to varying degrees in other nations of the world. American colleges and Universities use the system devised by the national library, the Library of Congress (LC) with a different, often more academic focus, to the call numbers and subject categories. As many people throughout the world readily recognize, a good subject classification scheme is an extraordinary tool for finding the information needed.

In these systems, and there are many other schema employed around the world, the call numbers often possess some relationship with the subject. For example, in Dewey classification, a book on Ancient Persian History is 955 M292h and is categorized as Iran — History, while in the LC system, Persian History is DS 272-275 and is termed Iran — History to 640.

Most of a library's holdings for a given topic are grouped in the same place on the shelves. You can usually find more materials on the same topic by examining the shelves for other materials on either side of your chosen book, to the perennial delight of human browsers everywhere. These systems are an attempt to mirror the way people make generalizations about a given topical area and make category judgments that then are useful for locating the material.

These systems run into difficulty quickly when a given document covers a variety of topics. How do you handle a book that deals with both war and economics? Do you place it in the bin labeled "War," or in the bin labeled "Economics"? Sometimes there is a specialty category ("Armed Forces— Appropriations and Expenditures," for example) but sometimes no perfect category exists. The decisions about classification and placement are not always easy, and catalogers work with rules and guidelines but often still make choices that are open to question.

When they are properly applied and the item in question does not have some built-in ambiguities as to its nature, the categories are often supremely useful. Good subject terms really do help to find relevant material, especially if they are arranged in a logical order.

But subject terms in library catalogs and other databases are created by thinking humans, not generated automatically by computers. The capacity of humans to think in broad symbolic terms makes them far better for arranging hierarchies of categories than machines, whose obsessive and thorough attention to discrete details makes them more suitable for other kinds of classifying activities.

With the Web, you also have a whole additional set of issues.

Web documents have no classification scheme at all, and despite the existence of some standards (the Dublin Core metatags), there will not be any such scheme anytime soon.

All the best classifications that do exist (Yahoo!, the World Wide Web Virtual Library, all the various specialty directories) are human-made. The amount of effort required to put them together (and maintain them, an often overlooked activity) simply cannot be applied to the entirety of the Web, and so the automated indexing of the search engines has become a second approach to finding information.

With automatic indexing, you have some advantages along with some drawbacks. As noted earlier, machines, at least so far, are peculiarly unable to recognize broad categories the way humans can. A document's content (its "message" or meaning) can remain quite elusive to a computer, unless the words contained in the document map nicely into good, usable categories.

What the computers are quite adept at however, are some capacities which humans do not do so well — recognizing and remembering the details. Automatic indexing takes advantage of this capacity, with a few wrinkles.

A Document's Nature

If all writers used only standardized terms, never employed non-literal mechanisms such as metaphors or similes, and only said what they meant in clear and unambiguous language (and never nourished any desire to deceive or distract potential readers) then distilling a document's content would be a much easier task. Standardized terms, ideally with a one-to-one mapping of word to meaning (i.e. one word would never have more than one meaning) would make the creation of an index much simpler.

Currently an Internet search for the keyword "cleavage" for example, delivers documents with multiple concepts. It retrieves entries whose topic is rock-splitting as well as information about shape enhancing lingerie. A change to one-meaning terms would eliminate this difficulty, although it would greatly impoverish a language, a point curiously irrelevant to our discussion.

The designers who work on automatic indexing rely on some basic assumptions—that the content of a given document can be derived given enough computing power and sufficiently sophisticated rules of interpretation. Some rules of linguistics come into play, that phrases and nouns with their modifiers are often reasonable representations of a topic. Computers are also capable of juggling all kinds of statistical information that can be put to use: keeping track of unusual words, which after all might be particularly valuable terms; how often a term is used in a document; or even how often per document size a term is used.

Even if these criteria were met however, it is not clear that automatic indexing would be sufficient in all cases. Abstraction and large pattern recognition are much more the province of humans than machines.

Database Design

All these index tables need to be organized so that people can search them. This part of a search engine's operation is known as the "back end," the part of the search engine that saves and organizes the information. Some of them are unbelievably large, but with computer data storage costing less and less each year, it becomes more feasible to offer good database features to searchers who will use them.

As of August 2001, estimates of the sizes of some major search engine databases have three with over a half a million pages: Google at 730, Fast with 552 and WiseNut indexing 510 million pages.* These

---

*http://notesss.com/search/stats/sizeest.shtml. Greg Notess, [Sept. 2001].

are very very large databases, and it takes some work to make the speed of a result's set fast enough to be useful. The actual searching does not go through these pages, only their representatives in the index tables, but increasingly there is some movement towards actual storage of these pages (Google does this by "caching" and saving pages, that can then be revisited, even after they have gone out of circulation) but this then means considerably more storage is necessary.

Databases have become part of contemporary life. Their presence saturates daily living, and your own personal information is stored in multiple places, in multiple formats. The U.S. government keeps records of citizens' employment information, along with data on residence, social security status and hundreds of other facts.

How these records are kept, arranged, "normalized" (corrected and cleaned up), and how all the different fields are linked, is now routine. Databases for Web indexes allow for flexibility and work best when they "scale" well, and can handle small and large numbers of records.

INTERFACE

An often neglected component of search engines (and many other applications) is the interface — the screen displayed on your computer that permits you to do what you want with the given application. A good interface makes searching easy. It should be well organized, so that little thought is required for navigation. It should be usable on all levels of computers, and not look different from Macintosh to PC, Netscape Navigator to Internet Explorer. Its language and layout should be clear and intuitive. Preferably, it should be simple, with lots of open space so that you can focus on the task at hand.

Alas, this is an elusive ideal. Crowded, confusing search engine screen interfaces make good searching more difficult. One of the

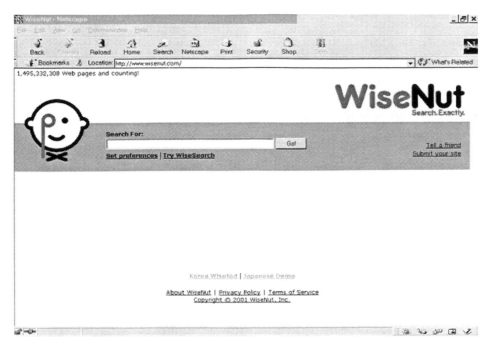

Example of a good clean Interface. http://www.wisenut.com/ Copyright © 2001 WiseNut, Inc.

appeals of the early Google interface, since grown somewhat more complicated, was its elegant, minimalist search screen. It was very clear to even the most unsophisticated computer user where to type the search terms, and what button to press to launch the search.

Commercial pressures now make many search engine interfaces a gaudy collage of advertising banners, marketing come-ons, and flamboyantly arranged pitches that would make a circus owner proud. When the search screen is buried amidst all the junk displayed, you have a pretty clear idea of the priorities for a search engine's site owner. For most search engines, the goal is not to help people find the information they need, but to make money helping people find what they need. Many times the public search engine is a showcase or loss leader for a company, who really would like you to make arrangements to use their services in a much bigger and more formal way, by contracting with them for your own company's Intranet search engine.

Much work in the field of Human Computer Interaction has been done to try to understand the issues behind good interface design, but as in much design work elsewhere, the number of decisions regarding overall layout and functionality of a screen make for tradeoff situations.

While one of the general principles of interface design is that lots of "white space" is good to reduce clutter, an overly minimal screen means that a user might have to make many more mouse-clicks to arrive at what they want, and thus perhaps be less practical or efficient. Designers continually balance the sometimes competing needs of the user along with the desires of the site owner, not always to the user's advantage.

Indexing images found on the Web presents interesting challenges. How do you arrange a collection of images? The crawlers can gather only a limited amount of information, perhaps the file title,

Non-text Files

As a quirk of Internet and computer history, the world of information is divided into two camps: text and non-text formats. Text is any file created solely by your keyboard (using any of the 256 possible characters—the ASCII set, which includes letters and numbers, punctuation marks, and some other special but standardized characters). Examples are most email messages, web-pages (which can include non-text files such as images, but whose basic structure is a text file), and documents created in simple editors such as Notepad for Windows or Simpletext for Macintosh users. Word processing applications such as Word and Wordperfect use a number of non-standard formatting characters that are hidden to users, and their files are non-text. All word processing programs have the option of saving files as text-only. One of the mechanisms that contributes to the crawlers' speed (vs. a human "surfer") is that they are looking only for text and do not bother to "read" images, which tend to be much larger, and hence slower, files to load when accessing a Web page.

its size and format (*jpg* and *gif* are the common formats found on webpages) and with a little work can deduce other features, perhaps color. But automatic indexing of a collection of, say, animal photographs is very problematic without metadata — descriptions of the work. The title of a given image file is probably the single most important quality, one reason to give your own files clear, intuitive names.

QUERIES

When a user usually thinks of a search engine, the query itself is often the first thing envisioned. You call up the URL of your favored search engine, type your topic words into the handy little text-box the search engine provides, press the "search" button and the little monster of a search engine goes off and brings you back a list of items for your perusal. Sometimes the list even resembles what you were looking for.

At this stage at least, your keywords are the only thing the search engine has to work with. This is why we will spend some time in the next chapter examining the process of choosing good keywords for a query. The search engine then engages in a matching game. Your chosen keyword(s) are checked against the multitude of index tables its crawlers have already created, and the resultant index records that match your query are returned.

Generally, your happiness with a given search engine is dependent on how well the search engine continues to retrieve documents relevant to your chosen topic, and how easy it is to use.

In typical computer culture fashion, there are essentially two main ways to query a database created by the crawling programs, with the common goal of presenting the most "relevant" material first in the list, the least relevant last. These are **Boolean systems** and those employing non–Boolean mechanisms. In practice, many search engines can accommodate both Boolean and non–Boolean queries, but not at the same time.

The Boolean system uses a common mechanism to evaluate "likeness" by term matching and set combinations, while all other systems use different mechanisms, with such extravagant names as "**vector space**" and "**probabilistic**" systems. In practice, there are hybrid systems as well, which include features of each.

With the assembled index information and your keywords in the query, the search engine now has to know how to make sense of it all. This perhaps is the key feature that makes for search engine success, particularly since result sets from the Web tend to be so large.

There is more than one way to go about ranking a retrieval set, and users usually will not be able to tell very well exactly what is happening that makes their list of documents get ordered in a particular manner. The ordering depends greatly on how the index tables get put together, based on the data the crawlers have harvested. Also important is whether the keywords are weighted or just assigned binary values.

The best case, of course, which always seems elusively rare, is when your search hits the bull's eye, and the first few documents you get are all right on target, exactly the kind of item you are looking for. We will look at the two dominant types of retrieval mechanisms and how they work, Boolean and non–Boolean systems.

Boolean Queries

Many Internet users are already familiar with this particular brand of posing queries, and it is also used extensively for other computer functions, notably circuit logic in computer hardware. Named after George Boole, a 19th century English mathematician, this model of set logic uses various attributes of a document, which when combined serve to make a set of similar items.

The three basic functions of a Boolean system include the functional operators AND, OR and NOT. By these three commands, terms can be used to characterize a given set of documents. (See the search logic section in the next chapter for a further, and more practical, discussion).

Besides the reputation developed over their relatively long tradition in computer circles, Boolean systems have the advantage of being relatively easy to program and quite fast. Their drawbacks include the use of rather inflexible syntax when constructing a query, and an irritating capacity to either return sets with nothing (or next to nothing) or a huge quantity of unordered and often quite unuseful documents.

Extended Boolean systems add some features that help return relevant documents. Some modifications include proximity connectors (making an AND only if terms are within a certain number of words) and weighting terms (giving greater value for a term used in a title, or by its order of appearance in a search query).

Non-Boolean Queries

Several varieties of non–Boolean systems are currently in use. They generally attempt to treat queries in the same manner as the documents themselves, trying to make best matches between the two.

Among other features, they employ "**natural language processing**" allowing queries that do not have to be constructed under the fixed (and sometimes awkward) Boolean formulas. They have some interesting characteristics that show considerable promise for future search engine design.

The vector space model is an attempt to make a three dimensional "document space" where documents of a similar nature are automatically "clustered" together. Documents are considered similar by calculating a theoretical "distance" between them, by means of trigonometric computations that measure the vectors of their index terms. The notion is that if one particular document is deemed valuable, finding others in its virtual neighborhood with similar characteristics would also be useful.

Another system evolved from the vector space model is the probabilistic model, which attempts to refine even more the concept of document "likeness." Instead of constructing a possibly arbitrary "document space," the probabilistic model attempts to automatically identify other documents with the greatest probability of being like the query posed to the search engine.

In a well-tuned probabilistic system, the probabilities are generated by the user's own decisions regarding document likeness. The opportunities for **relevance feedback**, which allows a user to tailor their first search into a more precise second search, is greatest for this system. The general idea behind this system is Robertson's "Probabilistic Ranking Principle" which maintains that results should be listed in decreasing order of their probability of relevance, i.e. "best stuff first."

One of the hallmarks of these non–Boolean systems is that terms are generally given weights, rather than the simpler "yes/no" approach of Boolean systems. The weights can be calculated by several different methods, including word order (first is greater), word rarity, and placement in the document. This improves the chances of at least some documents being retrieved for every query, rather than the unfortunate tendency of Boolean systems to frequently return null sets for a query. Search term syntax is easier, and many users find the natural approach of listing the first terms they think of on a given topic to be a profitable search strategy.

Advantages of the non–Boolean systems are several: queries are easier to formulate and often more flexible in their result set. The lists returned can be "ordered" in terms of their likely relevance. Results are often not quite so often the hit-or-miss affairs as with Boolean systems. Some of the advantages of these systems have been incorporated into some of the more standard Boolean systems that search engines employ, which can mean weighting terms and giving greater importance to term proximity. Much development work is still required for all of these systems.

RANKING AND ORDERING RESULTS

What are some of the ways a system designer might decide to rank their collection of items? Several methods that lend themselves easily to computer manipulation include facets such as these:

Number of occurrences. If a document mentions "parachute" forty times, it probably will be more "about" the topic of parachutes than a document that mentions "parachute" once.

Occurrences per document size. If you have a 500 word document that mentions "parachute" 10 times, it probably is more about parachutes than a 10,000 word document that mentions "parachute" twenty times. In the latter case, only a paragraph or two may deal with the topic, while the first document is much more likely to have parachutes as its central theme.

Proximity. In multi-term searches, generally a short distance between terms makes for a more relevant result. If your search engine handles "golden parachute" as two terms (as some do) your best results are going to be ones that rank documents with close proximity ("golden" followed immediately by "parachute") higher than just counting occurrences elsewhere in the document.

Where the term is found: If a given word exists in a title or document file name, the chances are the document may be more centrally focused on that term than another document with a different title. This assumes the title is reflective of a document's content, not usually a misplaced notion.

A file named "parachute" probably has something to do with the topic of the same name, although this assumption is abused regularly by the spammers. This quality is particularly true in databases of news articles, where titles are quite significant. A word found in a title (or perhaps in the first paragraph) will be assigned a weight greater than the same word found elsewhere in the document.

Overall term rarity. An education database will have certain words repeated over and over in virtually all of their documents, terms such as "learning" or "education." These terms have a somewhat degraded value as search words in this particular collection, while a rarer term like "subtraction" would be more likely to only appear in documents relating to "mathematics."

No. of documents

Precision

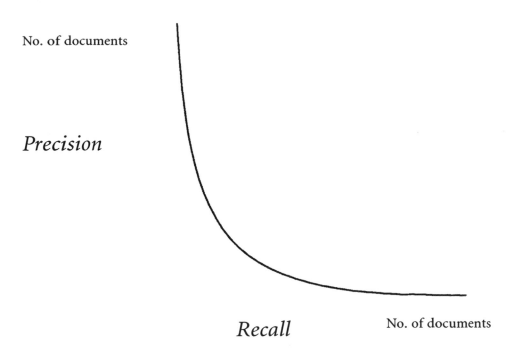

Recall   No. of documents

Normal document distribution for a given query showing the inverse relationship between Precison and Recall. The larger the number of documents retrieved (Recall) the fewer those documents will be relevant (Precision).

One of the time-honored axioms of the Information Retrieval field is the inverse relationship between **Recall** (amount of stuff found) and **Precision** (how relevant the information is). Do an Internet search on the American Civil War and you will be astonished at the volume of information located, some of it even perhaps helpful to your initial query. Do a search on the influence of Buddhist artwork on Manichaean bookmaking, however, and you will have a much smaller but more focused collection of information to work with.

OTHER SEARCH ENGINE FEATURES

Some other interesting features have been utilized by Web search engines that have received some attention by those in the field of

Paid Inclusion and Placement

One nefarious result of commercial pressures on search engine performance has to do with two practices: paid inclusion and paid placement. Paid inclusion is the means by which a creator of a Web page or site, its company or marketing department, will pay a fee for inclusion in the search engine's database. Since crawlers are not instantaneous, it might take several weeks or months before a new page or site is discovered and entered into a search engine's database. By paying a fee ("registering"), a website's address is thrown into the mix, where it thereby can be found by someone looking for it. If the goal is gaining visitors, for buying goods or services, or any other reason, a Web designer will want as many different access points as possible, and will register with all the major search engines. The pages still need to be well assembled, with good descriptive terms in the text, but paid inclusion speeds up recognition, and is very important to many sites.

Paid placement is sheer evil, however. Rather than paying a fee to register, paid placement is an attempt to bump a page's ranking up in the index order. For extra money, your site can be listed more prominently in retrieval sets. This is the major function of one company Overture (formerly known as GoTo), which then sells its lists to other search engines such as AltaVista, Hotbot, and AOL Search. This distorts retrieval sets and leads to skewed results, all of which is very bad news for users.

Information Retrieval. One feature is a notion called link analysis, which is a spin off of a practice used by various academic journal indexes. This practice works off the assumption, invariably true in academic circles, that if a given document is mentioned in other papers it probably merits greater "weight" in the profession than if it is mentioned not at all. Highly significant scientific papers are mentioned in the footnotes of dozens of succeeding papers.

A further refinement, made more meaningful by the size of the Web and the ease of link inclusion in Web documents, is utilized by Google and increasingly some other search engines by counting these links, providing a "popularity" count of importance. A document which is "pointed to" by a hundred other documents is assumed to be more important than an orphan document.

Sergey Brin, one of the founders of Google, describes this as taking advantage of the "topology" of the Web. Good information is noticed by the online world, and this recognition is often reflected in the links created to point to that document. This effort can be pushed even further by giving different weights to domains.

The frequency of cross linkages in the ".com" domain does not always mean quality information. If John runs an online firm selling shoes and someone else runs a site selling socks, it would be a natural relationship to each link to the other's page, although the cause of such linkage might not be the most objective in the world. But links provided by an ".edu" or ".org" domain generally have none of these commercial pressures and are more likely to be objective in the classical sense. Hence links from "princeton.edu" are very likely only made to quality documents.

RELEVANCE FEEDBACK

Good search engines are characterized by their ability to help you find good material. One significant way they can accomplish this is by what is known as relevance feedback.

Everyone has done a search on a topic and gotten a list of, say, ten items, of which perhaps one or two are deemed good quality for your purposes. A good search engine will be able to allow you to run another search to find more documents like the one(s) you chose.

There are a couple ways to do this. A few search engines, notably Google, AltaVista and Metacrawler will often have a link to "similar pages" or "More Like This." These link to collections of documents that resemble the one you have picked. The documents perhaps share a lot of the same terms, or are related by author, concept or perhaps even linkage similarity.

More on Spam

Spam, the unwanted dross of Internet life, causes search engine designers no end of grief. It is hard enough to develop indexing mechanisms for documents and adequate query paths for retrieval under the normal stressors of Internet size and diversity of documents, but when willful deception occurs regularly, indexing becomes extraordinarily difficult.

Why would this happen? Why should deception become the rule of life on the Internet?

The answer to this is multifaceted. Despite the much commented upon "dot com bust" of recent years, there is still a fortune to be made with Internet-based businesses. The limits of online commerce have barely been imagined, let alone approached.

Spam is a marketer's dream in one very important respect—its cost is a fraction of advertising using traditional methods. Newspapers and journals, radio and television—all charge impressive fees for advertising time and space, the revenues of which allow them to stay in business. Increasingly websites have adopted the practice of charging for advertising, as evidenced by the growth of "banner" advertising and other ads.

One dodge around paying for your advertising pitches is the practice of mass emailing and the deceptive indexing of websites.

Plenty of work has been done on email mass-mailing filters, which can help diminish (but not prevent) unsolicited, commercial emails. The mechanisms of deceptive Web pages is another matter, however. In organized environments, they are unlikely, but its practice is on a precipitous increase on the Internet. In libraries, standards exist for the cataloging of books, videos, audio materials and the like. But if you imagine a library that has no standards and allows the author (or the publisher) to "catalog" their own works, you get an idea of the difficulty. Nothing would stop an author from listing his latest work in a category deemed more attractive (for sales) even though a more objective viewpoint might put it elsewhere.

UnEarthIt!: A Hypothetical Search Engine

Let us consider a hypothetical search engine. Our outlandish model of a search engine is an attempt to examine some of the issues present in search engine design. The goal is to provide a kind of understanding that usually proves elusive to the users of search engines, who often neither know how their chosen tool is working nor why it delivers unusual or unacceptable results at times.

Here is our scenario. You are a smart, mathematics oriented young graduate from college, with no lack of confidence. Your wealthy but disorganized uncle Max has just died and left you his auto dealership and its parts department is yours to make a profit, if you can do so. Unfortunately, the entire parts staff has disappeared, you know next to nothing about the world of auto parts, and there are tremendous pressures to come up with a plan quickly.

The major goal: make the big warehouse of parts searchable so that inventory can be sold, the quicker the better to raise funds. Your own overwhelming confidence gives you notions of grandiosity and urges you to make a really good system, that can be adapted to bigger and better situations, with future corresponding wealth to accompany your progress. You need to figure out what you have in the warehouse, make a catalog so that people can find what they want, and then make it as easy as possible for customers to retrieve what they want, all so that dollars pile up more quickly.

The first necessity is to figure out what you have, and your present records are next to useless. How to do an inventory quickly and accurately enough for your needs? How can you balance the need for a truly comprehensive inventory vs. one that will be most useful to most people?

There are two possible approaches, which illustrate the tendencies of real world Internet mechanisms. You can go comprehensive, and dispense with any preconceived notions of the collection's order, and try to get a little bit of information about every item, with the hope that the information collected with help suggest the overall order of the collection on its own.

Or you can go with the advice of parts experts, who will look more selectively and with greater understanding of the items, but who will deliver necessarily a smaller if perhaps higher quality catalog. If you chose the second option, you will make a directory and have the specialists do the work of cataloging and arranging the collection.

But you go for the first option, and turn to a crowd of local teenagers for your indexers, whose main assets are speed and energy. You hope your plan will not require their maturity or intelligence, since both are in short supply. Their instructions are simple: comb the warehouse and record the parts information for the purposes of putting together a catalog.

What will they use for data? What is written on each and every parts box as a label. This includes a parts name, a number (which is factory supplied and unique to each part) and description. You will get back to more details later.

(Our carefully constructed search engine metaphor breaks down at this stage — if your warehouse were really the Web, your teenaged crawlers could only make their way through the piles of parts by following hyperlinks from one part to another. Each part would need to "point" to another related part for your indexers to make their way around the warehouse. Some automotive parts schema have the seeds of this approach by having groups of parts (brake parts for example) possess the same numerical prefix, but none of them operates like the Web, which requires that the crawlers only travel from link to link. Back to our metaphor).

The crew is off, dozens strong, and back quickly with their recorded information. This data is put into one big long list, and the fact that each part has a unique number means that duplicates can be discarded. You quickly codify the list so that numbers and descriptions are connected, and then send a second crew out to gather more data about your items. This second crew goes into more detail, hoping to gain some sense of how to organize the whole big mess by clues given out by the items.

This crew adds some other detail — how big each part is, its color and rough shape, but most importantly, they look at the parts number and examine related numbers. Perhaps all items related to the engine's oiling function have a number prefix (031) which makes it possible to ally them in your list, even though their actual (physical) location is someplace far apart.

All this data makes for a separate list, which gives a much better idea of what the actual item is like, but each item is linked immediately to the first list, with its location information.

Once compiled, these lists then make a searchable collection of records. They are not the items themselves, but merely representations of them. And they have "pointers" as data in their record that point to their actual location so that they can be retrieved quickly.

Now, the task is to make the whole business searchable.

For speed and universal access, you make a 24-hour computer terminal available. Users can type in descriptive words for whatever it is that they need, and your high speed computer will quickly comb the various lists to come up with a best match for the terms requested. It will provide the exact physical coordinates of the item so that it can be quickly found. (Here again in the real world of the Internet, this process is even better — your coordinates are your item's URL, which is then just a click away).

There is some really good news for this operation. The fact that your catalog is available all the time, every day of the year, is really darn nice for your potential clients. No opening hours, no closing hours, no limits on what can be requested.

It has some bad parts though too. Someone needs to know how to get to the computer, and then also learn just the best way to go about asking it for what is desired. In the interests of automation and the speed that comes with it, there is no person around to help you figure out what you want or need. You have asked your brightest teenager to write some guidelines to using the index, but his efforts have been marginal — he provides a perspective that does not know the forest for the trees.

You are capable of doing a search on "oil filters" and getting a huge list of items, everything from something that fits a 1934 Packard straight eight to a brand new Volkswagen Jetta four cylinder with a turbo. But, if you know what you want and know how to ask for it, you get a good part each time.

Even better, there are some self-correcting elements to your set-up. If you didn't include all the right words in your request, you still get a list of items for which your terms match, and it is sometimes possible to pick what you want from that list of returned items.

If you make this thing work, you may really be onto something. You can apply your army of teenagers to other situations. Their expertise is not required, only that they continue to comb through collections, collections of anything. They need to gather data, but your basic assumption, the only thing that makes this possible at all, is that there is enough data spelled out for each item that it can be recorded, and that you can organize it all into a searchable whole.

Results are best when the records of your items are full of good data, like the auto-parts are. Your index quality makes a huge difference in how well your catalog will work.

If you are really smart, you will keep track of traffic at your site and notice that everyone keeps going to one brand of oil filter more than any other, and you tweak your catalog to reflect this—any simple request for "oil filter" now gets this most popular one listed first, playing the probabilities that this is going to be a user's first choice.

You look at your whole collection, keep testing and keep looking at areas where your index is weak—can you somehow get more information about the items into your index? What is it about some searches that never seem to work right? Can you come up with better measures of likeness?

But when it works well, people are happy. They have a new set of skills, a newly found power of self-directed study, a range of retrieval not possible in older parts warehouse models, and best of all, the more they use you, the better you get, as the links build up and traffic makes some well worn paths to parts.

UnEarthIt! is a raging success.

3
Where and How to Look

*The difficulty in most scientific work lies in framing
the questions rather than in finding the answers.* —A.E. Boycott

GOOD SEARCHING

What makes for a good search? What makes for a good searcher?
The variations are enormous when it comes to searching behavior —
there is no one way to do things, although there are good practices
that are universally helpful. We are not precisely sure what qualities
make for superior searchers — some of these gifted beings seem to be
born and inherently possess unique ways of thinking and conceptu-
alizing ideas and topics.

It is tempting to think that through our long heritage as hunter-
gatherers we have assembled a set of survival skills that also end up
being particularly handy for Internet researchers: the ability to recognize concepts, distill essentials from complexity, and perhaps most
importantly, think on the fly. The ability to trouble-shoot a query
and take a different tack when the first salvo does not work is fairly
vital for success.

Good searching behavior can be considered to proceed in four
distinct phases. The first choice is one of location — where you will
look for your information. The second phase involves deriving good
search terms, which usually means considering your topic or question carefully. The third phase involves framing your question into

a format your chosen search engine can handle — posing the query. Fourth, you need to evaluate several things — is your result set of acceptable quality? Did your search capture your desired information? Do you need to rethink your question or somehow modify your initial search?

We will look at each of these phases sequentially. In the first phase, if you decide to explore with a directory, you can dispense with phase three along with some of the complexities of posing a query, and move straight to an evaluative phase. You will still need to consider terms in a second phase, although perhaps not as rigorously as when using a search engine.

You can often do fine by having a capacity to "recognize" good terms in a subject hierarchy, even if you could not generate them on your own. The browsing behavior suggestions also are relevant to phase four, as the process of viewing lists of resources and making discriminating decisions is an important evaluative component. Having posed a query to a search engine, you will be confronted with the results of your search, although in a less stratified way than as customary in a directory. If you have decided to go with a search engine, then the other phases of your process proceed in a linear fashion — you choose a starting place, pick some terms, pose your query and then begin the cycle of evaluation that may lead to repeat the steps again, until you are so exhausted, satisfied or bursting with knowledge that you need to take a break from the excitement.

LOCATING INFORMATION

The Internet has often been compared to a vast sea of information. It also has been described in less flattering terms, "cesspool" being an occasional epithet, with all of the attendant characteristics — murky, confusing, undifferentiated, intimidating, worthless. Finding what you want has always been a challenge, and knowing where to start has often been one of the major first steps for anyone in search of information.

While we are convinced that humans have developed over thousands of years a fascinating and quite flexible background of searching qualities, which have enabled us as a species to find food and shelter throughout the world, there are some attributes of the online world which make our normally robust faculties sometimes halting or ineffective. Computers continue to confound a great many people — their logic, although human-derived, is not always human-like.

The development of **Graphical User Interface** (GUI) browsers like Netscape's Navigator and Microsoft's Internet Explorer have contributed in heroic ways to the ease of use of the Internet for novices and experts alike by employing graphical representations. These visual methods allow certain data to be shown more clearly, and can allow for improved and clearer navigation around a given site. The point-and-click methods are speedy and quite intuitive compared to the older command line methods of online databases. Spatial representations of actions and items make navigation a far, far easier world than the methods that greeted new entrants to the Internet bandwagon ten years ago.

A fair amount of research energy is currently going into spatially oriented maps and ways to make finding information a more visual activity, and less dependent on fickle human memory or quirky organizational schemes. This is clearly an arena that begs for further study, as the visual processes of humans are so important in many other areas of life. Search engine designers have only just begun to explore better ways to represent result sets and provide easier paths to location.

We have looked at how the search engines operate, and how they go about attempting to catalog information so that it can be found. Some attention should be devoted to location however, since this is often useful in a number of ways.

In real life situations, we are often more effective at thinking and choosing when we are not in a sensory overload situation. Saying "yes" or "no" to a question is generally easier than providing a nuanced middle-ground response. Choosing between right or left when arriving at a fork in a country road is easier than picking which of five intersecting roads will carry you to your destination in a crowded, noisy city intersection.

There are times when the best course to pursue is to get your-self to a place with a good reputation for quality information in your topic area, and then browse, looking at and comparing sites until you have a clearer idea of what will satisfy you. Directories usually take advantage of the kind of value-added benefits that humans pro-vide any collection of information — they are reviewed and selected by humans, often ones who have a fair amount of specialized knowl-edge in that area, and consequently are generally of fairly respectable, even superb, quality.

Not all that long ago the world was fairly drastically divided between true search engines (Alta Vista was an early example) and directories, Yahoo! being the first major example. Over time, each type has incorporated advantages of the other, so that now Yahoo! incorporates the use of a search engine as well (Google is the current

Information Overload

Information overload is a condition experienced by increas-ing numbers of people. While the phenomenon was first men-tioned in 1945 by Vannevar Bush in his famous article "As We May Think" in the *Atlantic Monthly*, long before our current data-glut, this saturation causes a number of issues for online search-ing. How do you select a good set of results when the returned items number in the hundreds or thousands? What is the rela-tionship between quality and quantity? Does a surplus of data result in saturation bombing of cognitive decision making mech-anisms in a given individual? Web searching is at times akin to traveling for pleasure. Very often, smaller is better. There are times when you want the big city and all the energy and choices available, but there may be other times when you want some intimate resources that do not tax your decision making prop-erties too greatly, but still satisfy by their level of quality. For any given topic, the size of the Web usually produces a surplus of documents rather than a paucity. Your specialized directories may have a higher proportion of quality than can be delivered by a search engine. Directories can function like your travel agents, and if you have some basic trust in their expertise, you can often have a most satisfying experience.

engine, although Yahoo! has used others over the years, most recently Inktomi) and search engines such as Northern Light have gone and applied subject categories to their results sets. Thus the distinctions between search engines and directories can often blur.

If the goal is for users to find the information they want, this combining of functions is not misplaced. Humans often conceive of information in interesting ways however, and attempts to standardize classifications of knowledge always leave room for dispute.

So your first choice then is where to look. You should consider, however briefly, whether the Internet and your trusty browser are really the best approaches for your little information foraging expedition. While the speed and range of the Internet are entirely seductive, you should remember that most of the world's recorded knowledge is still best preserved in a non-electronic, highly durable medium — the sculptures, monuments and material culture of the past, and most importantly, in books and records written or printed with good ink on durable paper with strong protective covers. With decent care, these robust information storage containers last for centuries, and make digital documents look singularly ephemeral.

Having decided on the Internet, however, let us begin our journey.

Organization

The two types of Internet locating tools present their information in distinctly different ways. Search engines take advantage of their computational muscle and wide ranging automated programs to compile large searchable indexes. Their range would be impossible if humans were directly employed, and so they benefit from speed and the sophistication of the designers who work on the retrieval mechanisms.

Directories, on the other hand, depend on humans, and the human capacity to look at things and group "like" things together. How we do this is an interesting and poorly understood area.

Directories by nature are hierarchical, and familiar to anyone who has used a library or arranged a collection of anything. The initial "bins" of information are big, and hold a range of subcategories, which further subdivide to narrower and narrower classes of materials. For example, Yahoo! has a category Arts and Humanities, which holds 26 subdirectories, ranging from Art History and Artists to Visual Arts and Web Directories. Some of these sub-categories are small (Criticism and Theory with 26 items) while others are huge (Visual Arts with some 13,000 sites).

Directories by means of their hierarchies serve as guides to the user — they direct us from big, broad concerns to increasingly specific areas of information.

Search engines start from the other end of the equation, and plan to take advantage of computing power and careful design to distill content from documents, amassing a collection of details that can be managed by the user. To greatly over-generalize: use directories for great big queries, or when your own thinking is not precise; search engines when you have a clear idea of what you want and have good search terms ready for use.

Browsing Behavior

Why is browsing so important? What is it about wandering your way through a group of items, making decisions about keeping or discarding, that seems so natural?

Why cannot we just ask for exactly what we want most of the time? Our clarity as individuals is so often suspect, it is a marvel we get through the day at all. We often do not know what we want, whether in trivial situations like eating out at a restaurant or in the big global questions that govern middle-of-the-night quandaries: what do I want out of life? Luckily we are much better at choosing a course of action when confronted with some options.

In our lunch date at a restaurant, we can scan a menu and make some snap decisions— the sandwich sounds more appealing than the soup, the curry better than the noodles. The ability to choose directions is likely wired into our brains from a very long evolutionary development.

Invertebrates are often capable of making seemingly very successful decisions based on the cues they are given regarding simple perceptions such as vibration or temperature. We are able to examine and sort a variety of factors when making decisions regarding our choices of information, food, mates, friends, political leaders, etc. Browsing skill is recognized in the online world and helps explain the success and popularity of directories like Yahoo! and the Internet Public Library.

Why do directories work so well? Their hierarchy tends to be intuitive, or at least act consistently in following a scheme. On one level they serve as maps—you can look at a directory and fairly quickly generate some notion of how it is laid out. And maps are useful in multiple ways—they give you an overview, they allow you to think more productively about where you want to go (and suggest scenic detours for this trip or the next), and often they help you figure out where you are before you even start for somewhere else.

Directories also serve as prompts for term selection. This is particularly valuable when you really don't know what you want. Bigger categories can be explored and narrower categories identified. A specialist term for your topic may pop up on a browsing expedition that can then be used profitably on a new query.

It is rarely a bad move to trust your instincts when browsing. There are sometimes difficulties, particularly in specialist directories whose layout is poorly designed and whose terminology is confusing, but in general following your nose will take you in a productive direction. At worst it often helps to clarify your own objectives.

For most types of browsing on the Internet, a systematic approach can extend your success. Obviously if one directory or other site is consistently helpful, having its URL stored in your bookmark file or otherwise saved for easy location makes for shortcuts when on the path of discovery. Increasingly, it even helps to make a webpage, stocked with well-organized lists of your own favorite hyperlinks to information. Bookmark files can easily get overcrowded, and a webpage is one solution to the dilemma.

Advantages of Search Engines and Directories

Search engines work best when you have a clear idea of what you need, you strongly suspect that the Web is a good place to find what you need, and you have some good terms to use. One time that search engines work particularly well is when you are trying to get back to a page you found before, but neglected to bookmark or otherwise note the location of the file.

With the right set of remembered words, sometimes even fragments, you can often get right back to where you were. If you are prepared to think on your feet and modify your initial search and have some acquired familiarity with your search tool of choice, you can often exploit their power nicely.

The search engines work less well if your thinking is at all vague or unfocused. If you lack terms to describe your topic, search engines results are quite capable of being disappointing.

If you are just beginning a search and really have no idea of what you might find or how to go about your journey of discovery, directories are invaluable. Browsing categories can often lead to promising directions for information, and provide better terms for your inquiry. By restricting your search to a limited domain, you often increase both speed and precision.

Directories also benefit from human thinking. Categories are human inventions—we can see large picture similarities and differences and make judgments about different materials and directions we may want to go. When specialists are involved in the choices, the capacity for learning becomes greater.

SEARCH TERMS

Assuming you have chosen a search engine as your vehicle, the process of distilling good search terms for your desired information is often key to search success. Seemingly a simple enough task, it is quite capable of dazzling you with complexities.

Curiosity does not always begin with a clear-cut definition. In our experience, curiosity begins with an amorphous interest, and only over time with some thought does it become a formulated concept that can be turned into a successful (or at least promising) query.

A good search starts with good words. This, of course, is much easier said than done, for words are one of the great attributes of our species and part of our bewildering complexity. In particular, one question dominates research practice and remains vexing for everyone sooner or later from childhood to maturity: how do you ask for something when you don't know what it is that you want? How do you describe your need for information?

In the academic world that we inhabit, superior researchers are often the ones who can think up the best, and most interesting, questions. Some of these questions are basic and simple, but unapproachable from normal directions: How did our universe form? Why is the sky blue? What is love?

Good questions are often ones that can be answered, and these are the best for research efforts. The capacity to think of words to describe an interest is both an art and science, and luckily responds to practice and experimentation.

The standard method to clarify an information need is to try to write it down as a question. (This mechanism even works fairly well for some search engines as an initial search, too). In particular when doing a research paper for publication or trying to handle a grant application, it helps to try to frame the topic as a question: not "I want to study the American war of 1812" but rather "what factors both political and economic were at work to set the stage for the war of 1812?" Some questions lend themselves to answers better than others.

Once your question is out there for examination, it is usually possible to refine it and distill the essential components. The more you can derive good solid keywords, usually nouns, especially if they are unusual or precise terms, the better your search is likely to be (and this is true regardless of your target database).

One of the things that the search engines do is discard a list of **stopwords**. For most queries, articles such as "a," "an," and "the" are quite useless. All prepositions and many verbs are as well, along with adverbs and adjectives, although frequently a phrase with an adjective and a noun make for valuable terms (e.g. "Etruscan Art"). Nouns are almost always the best.

Computer scientist Richard K. Belew from the University of California San Diego has made an interesting observation about search terms:

> KEYWORDS are linguistic atoms—typically words, pieces of words or phrases—used to characterize the subject or content of a document. They are pivotal because they must bridge the gap between the users' characterization of information need (i.e., their queries), and the characterization of the documents' topical focus against which these will be matched. We could therefore begin to describe them from either perspective — how they are used by users, or how they become associated with documents.[*]

Your creative abilities will often be challenged at this stage of selecting terms for your research. Finding alternative terms is often essential, and your ability to modify your initial search after you have gotten some results can lead to you to more desirable information. This is one area that search engines may make significant improvements over the next few years.

Already, Excite has a process that they have termed concept searching, which automatically provides some term mapping in an attempt to get you closer to your goals. A keyword will not only return exact matches, but will get documents relating to the "concept" of the term. This is accomplished by means of a subject term thesaurus, and an entered term will also use its matching term in the thesaurus as a query as well.

There are other systems that employ this sort of thesaurus for good term application. But finding good terms to start your search is perhaps the best thing you can do to assure success, maybe even more important than your choice of search engine.

Good terms are:

Multiple
Unique or unusual
Specific and unambiguous

---

[*]*Belew, Richard K. Finding Out About : a Cognitive Perspective on Search Engine Technology and the WWW . Cambridge, U.K.; New York : Cambridge University Press, 2000, p. 10.*

Spelled correctly
Serve to describe essential characteristics of your topic

Bad terms are:

Stopwords (see previous section)
Most verbs and prepositions
Spelled incorrectly
Common (try a simple search on "love" or "war" and hold onto
    your hat when you get the results).

More words are almost always better than fewer, precise terms always better than their generalist counterparts. It may help to think back and remember how the search engines are put together, that your search terms are going to be matched up with a set of index tables.

An unusual word will have a lower frequency among all the millions of words that are found in the index tables, and will more likely be attached to a document of interest to you. More words means you get a tighter net — fewer non-relevant materials will have that same combination. Synonyms are frequently vital, and the capacity to come up with alternative terms makes for superior searching.

Like many other affairs of life, a search can be approached from two ends of a continuum. You can start broadly and work your way into narrower and narrower categories, or you can start very specifically, and broaden as necessary. Some of this depends on what you want. In general, when you have a specific interest, you should use a search engine and apply exactly the terms that describe your topic.

If you have some choices about where to conduct your search (or have other limits such as language or format (movies, images, etc.) this can sometimes also help to narrow the field). Your keywords may work better in some locations than others, and your best bet is always if they are relatively unusual. Experienced searchers frequently think hard about their keywords, hoping to combine both good accuracy and uniqueness in their terms.

POSING QUERIES

Search Syntax

Phase three is the issue related to posing a query to a search engine — combining your keywords into a form that can be processed by the search engine. There are a variety of aggravating qualities amongst the search engines as a whole, but the lack of standardization in acceptable syntax is a major one. Some of this can be explained by differences in how the database itself is searched (Boolean vs. non–Boolean) but much of it is simply insolent. Requiring capitals for Boolean connectors is ridiculous by any standard, and many of the variations in syntax are petty and unnecessary.

The combination of keywords is fairly vital to search success. There is a fair disparity between the various searches that can be done

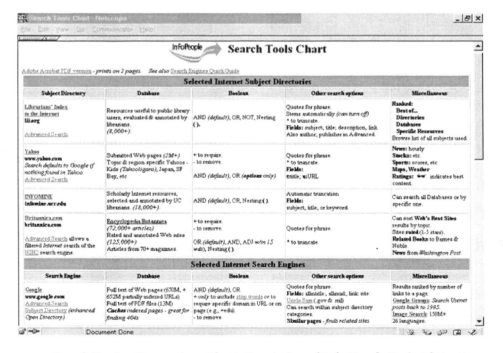

Search Engine Comparison Chart. Permission of Info-People Project http://www.infopeople.org/search/chart.html

with variations on the use of two keywords: civil and war. A phrase ("civil war" in most search engines) gets a much smaller and more relevant set than a Boolean AND ("civil and war"), an example of what happens when very commonly occurring words are used in a search, and even this is light-years improved over a Boolean OR ("civil or war") which is how Excite handles the request if just "civil war" is typed in the search window.

To try to keep the various idiosyncrasies straight, several different nice charts have been developed to allow a searcher to have a ready reference guide to search engine differences. Carol Leita has a good one at http://www.infopeople.org/search/chart.html. Two other good reference guides are Greg Notess' Search Engine Showdown at http://notess.com/search/features/, and Danny Sullivan's Search Engine Watch at http://searchenginewatch.com/.

Boolean Queries

Putting together a Boolean query can be an amusement of considerable vigor. The mathematical basis of Boolean queries is troublesome to many, but nonetheless, for a variety of reasons it remains the dominant paradigm for online searching. Terms are combined according to three distinct methods, and the Boolean "operators" as they are often called are AND, OR, and NOT. Much in the literature is devoted to the fine points of Boolean logic, so we will only outline the basics of Boolean searching. In our experience, it is often easier to understand Boolean logic by experience than by any particularly effective theoretical discussion.

The Boolean system has been in place for many years as a method of querying a database, and several generations of database users have grown quite proficient at coaxing maximum results from a Boolean query. Partly because of this accumulation of expertise, but also because using a Boolean framework often gives a searcher more control over the nature of the search posed to a database, many researchers prefer to use this method.

The choice and combination of search terms becomes an intriguing challenge, and the sense of power that accompanies a successful and difficult query has some appeal. Let us take our interest in steering wheels for Volkswagens and see what we can do.

With the list of keywords "Volkswagen steering wheels" we have three perfectly acceptable keywords. The words represents aspects of what is sought, they are descriptive, and a computer can process them. In the Boolean system, there are three basic ways to go about combining these terms.

AND

Search	Volkswagen and steering and wheels

If our search goes "Volkswagen AND steering AND wheels," we ask for a set of documents than MUST include at least one instance of each and every word ANDed together. With any luck, this means our document will be talking about steering wheels for Volkswagens. The usual graphic devoted to discussions of Boolean logic includes the mathematical diagrams designed by Venn to illustrate set theory. These Venn diagrams (dubbed "Zen diagrams" by wags in the field) look like this:

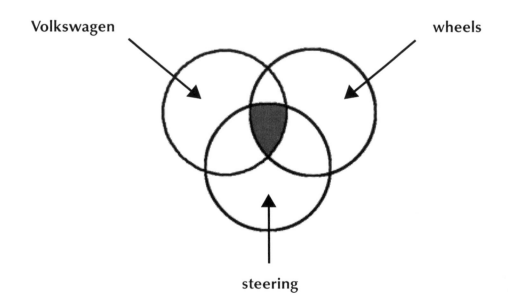

If your search was for the simple keyword Volkswagen, you would get an enormous set of documents, everything from the homepage for Volkswagen itself on down to Hot Rod Tony's Homepage which lists his collection of toy race cars, one of which is a Volkswagen dune buggy. Similarly your collection of documents for the keywords steering and wheel would generate huge sets of documents, all of them mentioning the keyword at least once in their text, thereby showing up in the database's index. By using the Boolean AND connector between these terms, only those documents that mention all three terms are returned, in this case a much, much smaller set of documents and (it is hoped) more relevant to the query.

OR

Search	Volkswagen or steering or wheels

The Boolean OR does just the opposite of AND. Instead of restricting the set of returned documents to those which have all three keywords, the OR connector returns items which have any one of these terms. Obviously, this expands the result set considerably. In practice, OR is useful when using synonyms (television OR TV) or variant spellings (labor OR labour, to get both British and American spelling versions).

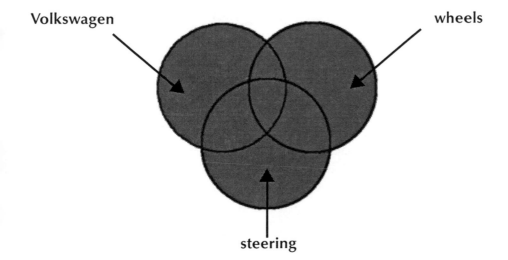

Volkswagen   wheels

steering

NOT

NOT, occasionally AND NOT in some systems, throws out one section of the set. If you want your search for Volkswagen wheels to disregard steering wheels, your search might look like this:

| Search | **Volkswagen not steering and wheels** |

This might not be the best search for this concept, but it illustrates what happens when you do an exclusion.

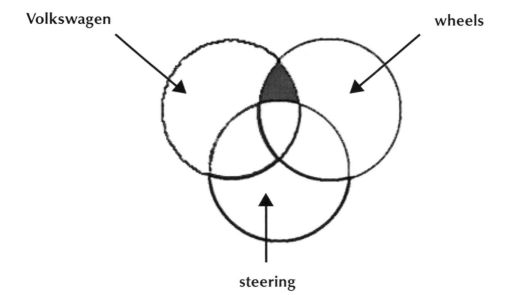

Excluding is often problematic, since while you may not be looking for "steering wheels" there may be perfectly relevant documents out there for you that do mention "steering wheel" somewhere in their text. This can be a little like tossing the baby out with the bathwater, but can sometimes save you a great deal of aggravation when your result set continues to be polluted by one set of documents with a nasty word you can then weed out.

In summary:

AND narrows
OR broadens
NOT excludes

While that is the basic theory, life can obviously get quite complicated. There are ways to construct very complicated queries with just these operators.

Supposing your hotel had an online order form for breakfast delivery (haven't seen this one yet, but it is only a question of time...) and you wanted whole wheat toast with jam, but didn't want the toast buttered first, and you would settle for any jam except blackberry, your request might look like this:

[(jam NOT blackberry) AND (whole wheat toast)] NOT butter

In this "nested" query, the searcher has insisted that the system process the sets in a deliberate order — get the set of "jam NOT blackberry," and the set of "whole wheat toast," find their intersecting (common) element and then make sure that set excludes the "butter" aspect.

It is not hard to see how other factors could make for a complicated query, when you start dealing with these nested queries, or those possessing other variations.

We will mention a couple of practical issues connected with this kind of keyword searching, and move onto other systems.

In practice, whenever it is possible to use a "phrase search" it is usually advantageous to do so. If you are after steering wheels for Volkswagens, you might not see the whole phrase together "Volkswagen steering wheels"(although this might not be a bad first start) but you would be much better off with a search that went

| Search | Volkswagen and "steering wheels" |

than our first example,

| Search | Volkswagen and steering and wheels |

The first will look for steering wheels as a concept, and ignore other sorts of wheels. The second could very well find documents that mention wheels and tires and in the same breath mention their connection to the car's steering mechanisms— not what you want.

[Just for comparison, in a trial run in a random search engine, the first search got almost 12,000 items. The second, and the third (not) around 2,000. With a phrase "steering wheel" the result was about the same as for the exclusion, although the set looked quite different in content. Numbers of course do not tell the whole story, since what interests you generally is not quantity but actual utility, but it does illustrate the properties of the different operators.]

The Boolean system is the most widely employed, but possesses some unhealthy drawbacks, not least of which is that it is cumbersome and does not usually reflect how people think about things. Its terms do not even correspond with the normal ways that language is used: if you were ordering salsa and guacamole with your burrito in a Boolean format, you would need to ask for "salsa OR guacamole" to get both. The tendency is also that very large sets of data are retrieved or very small (or null) sets.

Boolean queries are rather an all-or-nothing affair. Many of those in the theoretical reaches of Information Retrieval field detest the qualities of Boolean systems, but it has the advantage of being easy to program (and thus fast as well as easy on computing resources.) Regardless of its merits or lackings, it remains the dominant database query method, and a whole generation and a half of online searchers have grown proficient at maximizing search results through its use.*

Non-Boolean Queries

Does a non–Boolean system require a different approach for searching? The good news here is that most non–Boolean retrieval mechanisms are a lot easier for most people to use than the formalized

*For further information on Boolean logic from a practical standpoint, some nice tutorials have been put together. See SUNY Albany's site http://library.albany.edu/internet/Boolean.html by Laura Cohen, or San Francisco State University's Oasis tutorial by Maria Garrido and Jeff Rosen at http://oasis.sfsu.edu/chapters/Ch3/IC3a.html.

Boolean approaches we have just examined. In their most forgiving form they operate in "natural language" mode where questions can be posed in the same manner you would ask any person. Ask Jeeves is an example of a search engine that uses natural language processing. What makes this arrangement possible is a very large "discard" pile of stopwords.

Most of the time, non–Boolean language searching gives the best results when the following conventions are followed.

Use multiple words, the more the better, to describe your topic
Best words go first
Keep related words next to their kin

Non-Boolean systems are much more concerned with a matrix of terms, and can assign weights to terms to take into account a variety of different conditions. This becomes particularly important when it comes time to order and rank sets of results.

Queries

When you pose your first query, think of it as the beginning of a dialog. Like your mother always told you, you never know until you ask. The first query, rather than being a perfect formulation of your interest, can be a conversational opener. Like small talk at a gathering, you will learn more if you ask first (and it does make sense to ask intelligently, but you don't need to get so paralyzed by the process you end up never asking at all) and then listen carefully to the answer, which may give you better clues than your original thinking. Once a dialog is rolling, if you listen and modify your next round of questions, you are often able to learn much more, and much more thoroughly, than if you stopped with the first quick, impatient question.

One piece of advice ignored by nearly everyone until desperate need begs for attention is the use of a site's help screen. Virtually every directory or search engine worth its salt offers some sort of help, and occasionally these are extraordinarily good, providing not only basic advice about the search strategy needed at that site, but additional information about more complicated features of their searching mechanisms. Some help screens are so cryptic or minimal as to be nearly useless, but when visiting a search engine for the first time, it makes sense to pay attention to the help screens.

EVALUATION

Quality of Information

Many guidelines have been prepared over the years regarding evaluating quality, since this is a troublesome and persistent topic, but unfortunately no "check list" approach is adequate to insure real quality.* Quality remains one of the real drawbacks for Internet resources, and there are several facets to consider. The kinds of questions worth posing if quality is a concern include the following:

Who wrote the document and when?
What are the potential biases of the creator of the work?
What is the aim of the work?
Does the work have an internal logic that suggests it was carefully crafted?

In general, issues of quality do touch on several nagging concerns of Internet documents. The first issue is quite simple — authorship. It remains astonishing that so many webpages do not contain the slightest clue as to their creator.

For academic research, and presumably from many other perspectives, any document that does not have a clear author is in danger of not being taken very seriously. How can you begin to gauge the authority and reliability of a document if you cannot even determine who wrote it?

*Some examples of sites that attempt to grapple with some of these quality issues include: World Wide Web Virtual Library's section on Quality at http://www.vuw.ac.nz/%7Eagsmith/evaln/evaln. htm, UC Berkeley's by Joe Barker at http://www.lib.berkeley.edu/TeachingLib/Guides/Internet/Eval Questions.html and Hope Tillman's at http://www.hopetillman.com/findqual.html.

The only possible exceptions to this stance may be in the case of documents involving anonymous surveys, or connected to data (perhaps of a personal nature) for whom there may be good reasons to keep identities at a distance. The author's credentials may also play a strong role in establishing a document's credibility.

In university research the process of peer review has always maximized quality, but the closest thing to that on the Internet is a well-ordered and reviewed directory (the WWW Virtual Library site at http://vlib.org/ is one example), especially a specialized one. Automated solutions are sometimes helpful (Google's link popularity mechanism) but retain drawbacks and are hardly foolproof.

Even with thoughtful algorithms is a popularity count, however well-adjusted, always the best gauge of quality? Eventually you the searcher, need to define your acceptable level of quality desired and be very careful in how you apply your data.

Revising Queries

Your list of results from a search provides some immediate options. Search engines that do a nice job of listing results will give you enough information for you to gauge the item's utility. You should have a title and a URL at minimum, and the good ones will give you a quick sample of text, perhaps with your keywords highlighted (allowing you to see your terms in context), and sometimes some extra information, such as any subject categories they think your query fits into.

Other options may include a choice for more items of a similar nature ("more like" or "similar pages" or the like) or more pages from the same site. It is worth experimenting with these features in the different search engines to see which ones do a good job of leading you to other good resources. This area of relevance feedback, where your decisions connected to picking a given site or sites shape the next result set, is very promising for future development.

Often when you have found a good resource, you can pick up other good keywords for another search, or follow the hyperlinks from that page in productive directions. If nothing else, finding a relatively poor set of results might prompt you to rethink your initial query. What was unsatisfying about the set results? Completely irrelevant? Scattered? All commercial?

If you can identify what is wrong, perhaps there are solutions. If the junk is all from .com domains, perhaps you can exclude those from the next search. If your results are all scattered, can you determine why? If the keyword is one of those with multiple meanings, can you do a NOT exclusion (potentially valuable) or use a more precise term (better)?

Perhaps a different search engine is worth a try. If nothing else, this experimental approach allows you to see how different search engines process identical queries, and may pay dividends in the future, if not immediately.

Even for very good Internet searchers, the first query is not usually sufficient. It often takes a revision or two, and good searchers are adept at rethinking their searching goals depending on the results they get back from a first search. You are in good company if you take the time to think clearly and try again.

4
Search Engines

Men have become the tool of their tools. — Henry David Thoreau

Here is a short list of search engines, all included because they are either good, or have historic innovations, or are promising for the future. There are plenty more search engines, and all of their designers are hard at work to improve results.

The list includes some heavyweights (AltaVista and Google) some behind-the-scenes folks (Inktomi) and some new entries, some of which are barely out of their starting blocks (Teoma and WiseNut). We will briefly look at some metasearch engines, which harness a selected range of other search engines to provide a broader search experience.

GOOGLE (http://www.google.com/)

This is a good one. The founders have come up with a fine search engine, in many ways far ahead of everyone else, and the current standard to beat. They did it quickly and thoughtfully, and as an immeasurable bonus, have so far resisted many of the commercial pressures that have marred the products of other notable search engine companies.

Sergey Brin and Lawrence Page did the basic work as graduate

Google http://www.google.com/ © 2001, Google.

students at Stanford, and for several years as a beta-test version Google ran off a couple of old PCs in the proverbial Silicon Valley garage.* The goal early on was to make a search engine that could cope successfully with even very simple queries, and the overall design of the product reflects some very innovative thinking.

Once arrived at Google's search page, your first pleasant surprise is the relatively clean interface, just a nice clear screen with a minimum of distracting directions and links. In its initial phase, the interface was even more minimalist, but even as more content has been added, the clutter-free initial page is still effective.

The search window is a text box and has a button to click for searching. A legacy of the whimsical nature of graduate student projects is revealed in the existence of the "I'm feeling lucky" button, which has no explanation whatsoever. This choice leads you merely

---

For a "white paper" discussion of Google's theoretical framework, see the somewhat dated but still instructive paper at http://www7.scu.edu.au/programme/fullpapers/1921/com1921.htm, Sergey Brin and Lawrence Page, [Aug. 2001].

to the item at the top of your list of results for your chosen search, and if it really is your lucky day, perhaps you need go no further.

Google claims 1.6 billion pages indexed as of October 2001, but the numbers can be interpreted in various ways.* As with all statistical reckonings, the caveat "depends on how you count" reigns.† Regardless of how the number is figured, Google is one of the largest, if not the largest of the search engines.

A few things besides the interface make Google stand out. They incorporate some of the work done in citation analysis in other parts of the scholarly world (bibliometrics—the study of how academic journal articles that cite other works make a matrix from which it is possible to grasp the relative importance of a particular author or journal article) and apply it to the Web's peculiar and evolving structure, using the "topology" of the Web, as they call it. Google uses a modified "link popularity" algorithm that takes into account the domain of the citing source, giving greater weight to an .edu or .org domain than a .com domain. This is not a perfect solution, but one that does tend to weed out some of the commercial biases and agendas that tend to influence a page's importance. They do not sell placement in their list of results.

Some other highlights include spell checking (also employed by Alta Vista but very few others) which helps solve a remarkable percentage of searching errors, a phone book for business and residences, stock quotes, dictionary definitions and maps. You can search for images, and result sets give you options on each item for "related" sites and linked pages.

So far the only overt signs of advertising is a "sponsored" link at the top of a list of results, but at least it is labeled as such, which is not true of all other search engines.

Google can also search for documents in PDF format, a standard for a great many documents (the U.S. government produces a lot of their forms and other documents in this format, which requires

---

*See Danny Sullivan's *Search Engine Watch* for details. "The Search Engine Report," August 15, 2001. http://searchenginewatch.com/reports/sizes.html [Oct. 2001].

†A good article on size and numbers is also at this site, with some interesting comments on link analysis. "The Search Engine Report," Danny Sullivan, March 3, 2000. http://searchenginewatch. com/sereport/00/03-numbers.html [Oct. 2001].

a separate reader to view, luckily free from Adobe at http://www.
adobe.com/products/acrobat/readstep.html). Preferences allow for
an impressive array of features for customizing results, choosing a
particular language or applying a filter to weed out pornography.

They clearly use a non–Boolean system, which can accommodate simple Boolean queries as well. A few complaints include the
lack of truncation, or stemming (no wildcards), but their help screens
are extensive and well written.

NORTHERN LIGHT (http://www.northernlight.com/)

Northern Light is a favorite of librarians and other experienced
online searchers for a number of reasons. While their search engine
index is large and healthy, it also incorporates one feature that helps
greatly in the choice of quality or topic specific information.

A search done in Northern Light produces a list of results which
can be browsed by broad category. For example, a search on Buddhist
art can generate a number of categories in the returned list that makes
further choices potentially more relevant.

They claim to do this uniquely to each search, and in fact your
big list of results is really just put into a series of categories for browsing. Our search for Buddhist art, for example, had some 140,000 different items, but Northern Light grouped them into a few dozen
categories, which included "Buddhist art and architecture" but also
more narrow divisions such as "Korean Buddhism," "Chinese, Mon-
golian & Tibetan arts" as well as bigger categories like "Buddhism"
or "architecture." The overall result is highly pleasing, and for many
searches this sort of arrangement is helpful.

Their searches run over not only the portion of the Web that they
have indexed but include a "special collection" of some 7,000 full-
text publications, generally with fairly high quality content.

The layout of their search page is nicely done — full, but not
over-complicated. There is a little advertising at the bottom, but this
is done in a far less obtrusive fashion than most. They have a nice
simple text box with a search button clearly labeled.

Size, Again

Greg Notess* mentions a fascinating little check of Northern Light's size at any given time (369,149,210 items as of October 2001). If you run a query in Northern Light for "search or not search" (his example), you get a list of all documents in their index, since every single one of their documents will either have the keyword "search" in their text, or will *not* have the keyword "search" in their text. Why this ingenious trick does not work for all search engines remains a bit of a puzzle.

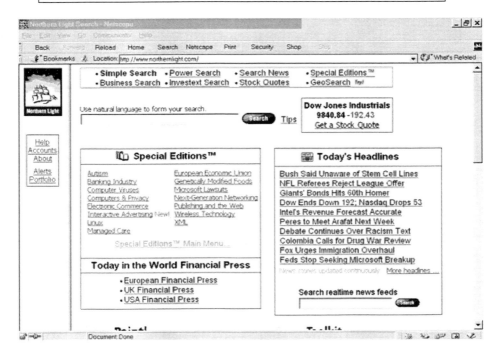

Northern Light http://www.northernlight.com/ Copyright © 2001, Northern Light Technology, LLC

Many options for limiting searches are available in their "power search" function, with options of searching by subject, type of Web site, and type of document (e.g. commercial, educational). Several specialized searches are possible, including business and stocks,

*http://notess.com/search/stats/0007sizeest.shtml, Greg Notess, July 6–7, 2000. [Oct. 2001].

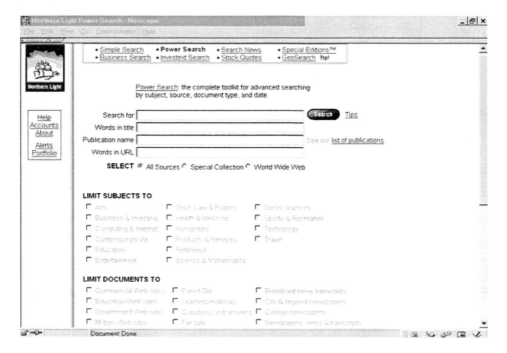

Northern Light Power Search http://www.northernlight.com/power.html
Copyright © 2001, Northern Light Technology, LLC

investment, and news. Field searches are unusually varied, and besides the ability to search by URL or title, other fields such as ticker symbol (for stocks) or company are available. Additionally, it is possible to issue a command that will sort the results by date, a nice feature.

Also useful is the very clear way that Northern Light makes the domain of the various results known: in bold letters it indicates whether the item is from an educational institution (edu) or a commercial (com) or government (gov) or other entity.

Unfortunately, as of January 2002 this site no longer offers free access.

ALTAVISTA (http://www.altavista.com/)

AltaVista entered the universe of the World Wide Web with a bang in 1995. They were first in a number of categories: first big full-text index, first multiple language searching capability, first with multi-language translation, which was especially unusual then for handling non–Latin alphabets such as employed by Chinese, Japanese and Korean, first with a spell checking function (very helpful for catching badly formulated queries) and one of the first to do a good job with image and non-text documents.

The first item, *full-text* indexing, is still a strong suit. By indexing whole documents rather than the abridged documents as was common with most other search engines in 1995, they went a long way towards putting together a nice index that would often get documents the other search engines could not reach.

Started by people at DEC (Digital Equipment Corporation), AltaVista was designed to be a showcase of DEC's technological innovations. Their power was unmistakably obvious when Yahoo! selected them as their exclusive search engine partner in 1996. But AltaVista has not fared well in the succeeding years of increasing competition

AltaVista Home Page http://www.altavista.com/ Copyright 2001. AltaVista Company, All Rights Reserved.

from other search engines. They were sold more than once, first to Compaq in 1998, most recently to CMGI, and seemed to lose focus after each change of ownership.

Their search page has grown increasingly cluttered over time, but at least it still retains a good long text box at the top of the page. A lot of options are right up front: choice of language, various formats or locations (images or news), an adult-content filter (on or off) or type of search (text only, search assistant or advanced). The latter choices are interesting, and offer searchers considerable flexibility in how they put together their queries.

"Search Assistant" (formerly "Power Search") formats the query boxes differently in a way that prods novice searchers into productive query directions, and possesses good date limiting functions. The advanced search gives the searcher options on how to sort results sets by specifying keywords in preferred order of weighting, more power in the construction of Boolean queries, and also gives good limits to date and language.

Like many other search engines, they have a set of subject categories at the bottom of their page, so they have assumed the look of a directory as well as a search engine. Unfortunately, the amount and flamboyance of the space devoted to advertising has grown intrusively since their beginnings, and AltaVista itself is only too happy to tell you about how to submit your own website for inclusion in their index for a price (only $39 for the first URL, but if you are going to add more than a hundred URLs, the price drops to $12 each, unless the pages are "adult content," for which you pay more)(!).* The name of the game is only too obvious.

Results are often good however, and their large full-text index is a big reason for this. They also do an excellent job at handling images.

EXCITE (http://www1.excite.com/home/search/tools_overview/)

Excite developed some innovations early in its existence. It was the first big company to use what they have termed "concept" searching,

*https://www.infospider.com/av/app [Sept. 2001].

whereby a thesaurus of terms is put between query and your eventual result.

The advantage of this practice is that a keyword you enter is "mapped" into a set of standardized subject headings, and your query can benefit from either more results (since you have used a standard term) or more precise results, since your standardized term was perhaps more precise than your original.

Results of searches can be uneven, with some very good right-on-target hits, but then the next search can be rather disappointing. It is not always easy to tell why (whether it just has not indexed the page you are after, or uses relevancy rankings that need more tweaking) but its relevance feedback feature (the "zoom" button) is often useful.

The search page is way too busy. Their layout makes it very hard to find various aspects of the search engine. The "zoom in" button is a nice feature, but until you look at the explanatory page, you have no idea what it actually does. In fact, with respect to the entire site, most help is inadequate. Advertising is distracting, particularly when blinking words or animation are prevalent.

Their advanced search has mixed results too. They have an interesting approach to keywords, with some choices about how much you want to "weight" your terms ("very important," "important" or "exclude"). Then they provide the option of a language box, a fine idea on its own, but you are limited to only a handful of languages, with English as the default and with no option for "all."

It feels like a search page slapped together with a number of different qualities that do not have much coordination between attributes. At least the advanced search page is blissfully free of advertising.

This is an example of what happens when a search engine with some good ideas (concept searching) fails to live up to potential. This could have occurred for a number of different reasons, but the result is less than satisfying.

HOTBOT (http://hotbot.lycos.com/)

Another interesting search engine is HotBot, which is part of the Lycos network. Lycos was an early Web search engine, now since become a large purveyor of Internet services. The backbone of HotBot's searching is outsourced to the Inktomi people, who make the actual search mechanisms. Inktomi is also used in a number of other venues, as they provide searching service to MSN, AOL and a fair number of other Internet portals.

Inktomi was an outgrowth of some research done at the University of California at Berkeley, and takes advantage of some advanced Information Retrieval practices, including probabilistic retrieval. They have elected to go after commercial accounts, becoming a behind-the-scenes mover and shaker rather than a star in the spotlight.

HotBot Search Page http://hotbot.lycos.com/ HotBot ® is a registered trademark and/or service mark of Wired Ventures, Inc. a Lycos Company. All Rights Reserved.

HotBot's directory is very prominent on its top page. The directory is a useful one, although more commercially oriented than many might prefer. With each choice of a category, you get a full screen's worth (five items) of sponsored sites at the top, which gets tiresome quickly.

HotBot's approach to editorial input on the categories is a classic Internet stance: it appears that their "open directory" is available for anyone to apply to become a category editor. This makes some sense, since human cataloging of Web resources will always be inadequate, and this way there is some attempt to garner quality of understanding in the construction of their directory.

The search box is simple enough, with preferences located on a sidebar. Their database is large, and was subdivided in 2000. They adopted a singular process by which a first search goes through one section of their database, then if results are unpromising, runs through a second, larger index.

The help screens are good, with solid information without an overload of detail. Results of a search fall into three categories: Top 10 sites, HotBot directory sites, and general Web results, although not every search will have all categories, and often only one. Additionally there are "featured listings" and "search partners."

The search partners choice simply takes your search keywords and plops them into the partner's descriptive generic sentence, which results in some ludicrous possibilities such as "Buy *college admissions* and save on shipping at Ecampus.com!" or "Great prices on *Australian aboriginal languages* at eBay." The awkwardness of the phrasing is a reminder of the goal of this, and most, search engines: profit.

One interesting feature of a HotBot search is that if your keywords happen to match a HotBot directory category, some of the results have an option to find more similar pages. The number of sites on the results list with this option often varies from query to query, for no apparent reason.

There is a fair amount of advertising on HotBot, which is especially distracting when there are blinking or animated advertisements with garish colors, a fairly frequent occurrence.

Their advanced search page has a dizzying array of modifiers, which include everything from format (pages that include images, javascript, video, etc.) to date, location, and language.

A wide variety of services make it obvious that HotBot operates as a portal, as there are a multitude of links to various sites. There are options for an email/white pages directory for people, and a large number of commercial choices (cars, hardware, books, etc.) as well as some useful other categories, maps among them.

ALLTHEWEB (http://www.alltheweb.com/)

AlltheWeb is an intriguing search engine partnership started by researchers from Norway who founded the FAST company in 1997 and Dell computers, who supply the computer hardware. They made their name doing good work with non-standard document formats, including various multimedia, and started with a very large initial index.

They earn high marks for making a very clean interface that is easy to use. A lot of thought has gone into their design of buttons, help screens, and choices for actions. They offer a wide array of customizable features, which allow a searcher a great deal of freedom about how results will be found and displayed. They have an anti-porn filter delightfully labeled "Offensive content reduction" which presumably dispenses with not only pornography but perhaps any other assault on your tender sensibilities.

WISENUT (http://www.wisenut.com/)

WiseNut's interface could not get more minimalist — it is a jewel of simplicity (see page 27). From the search page you have very few options, so the user generally cuts straight to the chase and types in some keywords. From the main search page, your only other options are to use a "WiseSearch" which is just a series of fields that allow you a little more control over the weighting, or the preferences page, where you can arrange your preferences to limit your search by language and a few other characteristics, including the use of their "Wisewatch," a pornography filter.

WiseNut claims an enormous number of webpages indexed, nearly 1.5 billion as of October 2001. There is no help offered at all, and the whole process is almost too stark for comfort, although the complete absence of advertising has such a redeeming effect as to make it stand out proudly among the other search engines.

Results are good, and list enough information, with your keywords highlighted, to be very helpful in deciding when to follow a link. Like Northern Light, they usually, but not always, break your results down into categories to help direct your path through the results set.

TEOMA (http://www.teoma.com/)

Teoma is the newest of our short list of search engines, having debuted in May 2001, although its history goes back to a Rutgers University project in 1998. Just when people were beginning to discover Teoma, it was acquired by Ask Jeeves in September 2001.

Teoma extends some of the same ideas that made Google so good — link analysis. When a search is run, Teoma does a link analysis and attempts to identify "expert" links within the "community" of results, and weights those "recommendations" more highly. The attempt is to give your results set a better (more authoritative) ranking. This works in two ways, by both tweaking results sets for potentially improved relevance, but also by creating some linkages within results sets, so that your search results may contain an "expert links" set of sites deemed especially valuable, which is clearly displayed in your results page. Like Northern Light, they also display a series of subject "folders" which allow you to browse through various categories or aspects of your results.

It runs well and shows promise, although it suffers at the moment from having a relatively small index. Its size will doubtless improve, and the acquisition by Ask Jeeves may give it options to move in more intriguing directions.

ASK JEEVES (http://www.askjeeves.com/)

Ask Jeeves was the first search engine to proclaim the virtues of natural language searching, which remains its most marked characteristic. Begun in 1996, it grew steadily and now counts as clients a large number of very prominent companies, from Ford Motor Co. to Nike, Dell and Compaq computers. Besides its natural language features, it employs relevancy ranking that is furnished by searchers' preferences, so that lists of results are continually evolving as their usage changes.

Ask Jeeves also employs human catalogers, who have created a series of topic areas for browsing, in much the same fashion that Yahoo! and Northern Light have done.

METASEARCH ENGINES

Metasearch engines employ a selected number of other search engines to run a search. In a sense they are middlemen, wholesalers, who send a search to their partners and retrieve the cream of the results.

In theory they are a good idea, since they should be able to take advantage of the combined strengths and indexing depths of a range of other search engines. In practice, they have some considerable drawbacks. Because they take one search query and translate it into a form that can be processed by each of their feeder search engine partners, there is often a loss of precision, particularly for all but the simplest queries.

Obviously, they will never be better than the *strongest* of the various partner search engines, and they can also deliver poor performance when the searches sent to the different partners time out (a fairly frequent occurrence) or have difficulties for any reason.

On the other hand, we know many people who are quite happy to use them, particularly on a first search. Since many people usually only look at the first page of results from a search engine's result set anyway, this approach gives a quick, broad look at a particular topic.

METACRAWLER (http://www.metacrawler.com/)

Started in 1994, Metacrawler was another outgrowth of a university project, from the University of Washington. Professor Oren Etzioni and graduate student Erik Selberg launched it in 1995, and it was one of the first of the metasearch engines.

Unfortunately Metacrawler has a very busy front page, but its results return fairly quickly. The following search engines are employed as its "scouts": AltaVista, DirectHit, Excite, FindWhat.com, Google, Overture (formerly GoTo), Internet Keywords, Kanoodle, LookSmart, MetaCatalog, Sprinks by About, and Webcrawler. Although this list is impressive, any given search will only be sent to a handful of the group. Even then, there are often reports back of at least one of the scouts "timing out."

Another drawback is inclusion of the commercial "pay per click" Overture, whose entire index is constructed of paying clients.

They often provide useful categories for further searches, *à la* Northern Light, but their "featured site" (a sponsored site) is a designation at the top of some result sets. You can also sort your result set by relevance (the default), site or source (the search engines employed).

The choice of formats is extensive, with images, multimedia, and newsgroups among other options.

IXQUICK (http://ixquick.com/)

This metasearch tool makes a very nice first impression: a good clean interface and the opportunity to use over a dozen, mostly European, languages, from Finnish to Turkish. Your choice of formats include Web documents, News, Movies and Images.

Results are cleanly listed, with enough information to help you decide whether to visit the site or not. Sponsored links are clearly marked and relatively unobtrusive. The help-screens are very good, and provide not only basic information but let you know clearly how to get the most out of Ixquick.

For searches on the Web, Ixquick utilizes AOL, AltaVista, EuroSeek, Excite, Fast Search (AlltheWeb), FindWhat, GoTo, LookSmart, MSN, and Yahoo. For their other formats, they utilize a smaller number of specialized search engines, which seems to work quite well.

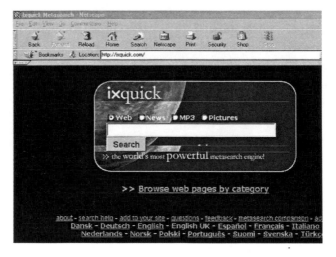

Ixquick. Reprinted with Permission of Surf board Holding BV, The Netherlands

5
Directories

*The brain's strong point is its flexibility. It is
unsurpassed at making shrewd guesses and at grasping
the total meaning of information presented to it.* — Jeremy Campbell

Libraries and other collections of information have been part of our collective heritage for two thousand years, and it is not unreasonable for us to apply what we have learned from making libraries and arranging collections of information to the new phenomenon of the Web. Internet subject directories often provide a very useful and high quality service by grouping information into categories that are both recognizable and practical.

Several good directories have been put together since the mid–1990s, and while there is still lots of room for better, fuller and more specialized directories, the ones that are out there are often supremely helpful.

Some common elements of the various directories include:

- Hierarchical approach to organization

- Consistent scheme of organization

- Standardized vocabulary

The main plus of the directories is that you are able to take advantage of some discriminating human evaluations. Good directories are put together thoughtfully, and generally decisions are made to include resources when they are 1) quality information sources, with authoritative creators, well written and clear, and 2) stable, and unlikely to migrate or change over time, often with proper updates.

Directories help you find things in ways other than the obvious path of leading you to resources. By browsing subject categories, you often can gather ideas for further exploration.

Perhaps you discover that the search terms you had used for a topic are outdated or inadequate. There may be more precise or current terms to use, or perhaps there are related terms that capture your interest a little better. The capacity to think more clearly about a given topic is often enhanced when you have some comparison materials to examine.

Directories also have the capacity to work both formally and casually. A good directory can soak up many pleasurable hours as you forage about its categories.

While directories take advantage of human indexing and decision-making, their authority, as in most other human endeavors, is not foolproof. The same commercial pressures that work to adversely affect quality in search engine results are also apparent in some of the directories.

Independent, non-profit (often volunteer) groups like the Internet Public Library or the World Wide Web Virtual Library are often more dispassionate and discriminating about the resources they choose to include in their list, but since so much of their labor is non-paid, the results tend to be a bit uneven. Some parts of the WWW Virtual Library are rich grounds for information while others are sparsely inhabited.

Your choice of directory may depend on the particular desire you are seeking to satisfy. If your interest is to find out more about a company or an online business or service, the WWW Virtual Library is not as good a bet as perhaps Yahoo! On the other hand, if you are looking for some online medieval texts, a good academic directory like the World Wide Web Virtual Library is a marvelous finding aid.

YAHOO! (http://www.yahoo.com/)

This was the first big directory, and still a favorite of a great many Internet denizens. It got started in 1994, while the Web was still in its infancy, and the story of its bootstrap operation by a couple of Stanford graduate students is part of the Web's growing mythology.

Two Electrical Engineering Ph.D. candidates, David Filo and Jerry Yang, had been assembling interesting World Wide Web addresses using some campus computers, and their list had grown so big and fast that it became necessary to organize it along category lines. Directories subdivided into subdirectories, and soon they filled up and were subdivided once again.

Yahoo!'s success took nearly everyone by surprise, but it clearly met an overwhelming need, and as the numbers of Internet citizens grew, its popularity expanded as well. The financial promise was so sudden and great, that Yahoo! was off and flying as a commercial venture within 14 months of its founding, as it incorporated in 1995, and the rest is what passes for history when dealing with the online world.

Yahoo! is now what is termed a portal, a place that offers a dizzying variety of Internet functions and services. More than an index, Yahoo! offers email service, bulletin boards, shopping locations, and, as has become the norm these days, it is plastered top to bottom with advertising.

At its top page, there are fourteen main categories which include Arts & Humanities, Business & Economy, Computers & Internet, Education, Entertainment, Government, Health, News & Media, Recreation & Sports, Reference, Regional, Science, Social Science, and Society & Culture. Each of these main categories subdivide into multitudes of further and more specific sub-directories.

Under the main category for Health, for example, there are 48 other subcategories, one of which is Diseases and Conditions, which in turn divides into almost another 50 subcategories. These frequently then contain actual site listings, although there may be more narrowly defined subcategories as well. Thus Skin Conditions has

Yahoo! http://www.yahoo.com/ Reproduced with permission of Yahoo! Inc. © 2000 by Yahoo! Inc. YAHOO! and the YAHOO! logo are trademarks of Yahoo! Inc.

both general sites but also more subcategories, with more specific focus, e.g. leprosy, eczema.

Yahoo!'s main asset is their sheer size and comprehensiveness. They have categories for just about anything you can think of, and have been responsive to what people using the Internet want in a directory. It is possible to run across out-of-date links, but for the most part Yahoo! is maintained very well.

THE WORLD WIDE WEB VIRTUAL LIBRARY
(http://vlib.org)

This is an example of a pleasant outgrowth and subset of Internet Directories: the virtual library. Ever since the Web made it possible to post documents for public viewing so easily, there has been a movement towards making more and more content publicly available.

Virtual Libraries are online collections, and their listings are usually not just long lists of websites, but include a preponderance of online collections. The WWW Virtual Library has an academic focus, and is oriented towards those engaged in college and university level research.

The WWW Virtual Library has roots that go very deep into the Internet's history, as it was begun by Tim Berners-Lee, a founder figure for HTML and the World Wide Web itself. Now coordinated by Gerard Manning, the WWW Virtual Library is a collaborative effort of a great many volunteers, who over the years have offered their expertise on a variety of subject areas that have Internet access.

After a day spent among the commercially driven search engines and directories, the WWW Virtual Library is a welcome relief. There is no advertising, and it is heavy on content, low on flash.

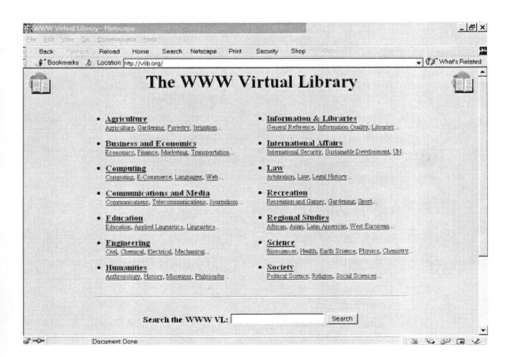

The WWW Virtual Library http://vlib.org

The top-level categories include Agriculture, Business and Economics, Computing, Communications and Media, Education, Engineering, Humanities, Information & Libraries, International Affairs, Law, Recreation, Regional Studies, Science, and Society. The information that is listed is of a very high level of scholarship and quality.

The Virtual Library volunteers agree to making quality the highest priority of their listings, making sure that each selected listing is "one of the best" in its area.* There are over 300 libraries included in its central database, but searching can be done both by keyword (in the full-text of the document) and by document title. Browsing is done either by the broad categories, or by an alphabetical list, a rather long and less useful approach.

Despite the nature of the collection and its volunteer basis, the currency of information tends to be quite good, and many of the libraries are maintained very well. The organizational scheme mirrors that of a research university, with broad, inclusive, often multidisciplinary categories. At the more specific levels the comprehensive nature of the Library begins to break down a bit, and there tend to be gaps of coverage at the second and third levels of classification.

The weak areas of the WWW Virtual Library are two: some of its material is quite old, which suggests that updating is a sporadic process, and its coverage is quite uneven. Both these drawbacks are clearly due to the nature of the endeavor: as a volunteer creation, the pages developed owe everything to the time and energy available from its participants.

The Librarians' Index to the Internet
(http://www.lii.org/)

This is another one of those fortuitous, almost spontaneous growths of Internet resources with roots that predate the World Wide Web. While a favorite for librarian-types, as its name suggests, its

*http://conbio.net/vl/database/admin/getlisted.cfm. [Oct. 2001].

utility is not limited to this group alone, but serves a wide range of Internet users.

The initial file was a bookmark of gopher sites (the upstart flashy tool that immediately preceded the World Wide Web as a finding mechanism, which was immediately killed by the phenomenal growth of the ease of Web graphical browsers in the early 1990s) that migrated to the Berkeley Public Library in 1993. Carole Leita, the founder and a reference librarian, kept improving the list, and three years later with the collaboration of Roy Tennant of the University of California Berkeley, established a durable and useful subject heading scheme and added a search mechanism. There are now over 100 librarians, entirely from California, who have put together the categories and stocked them with good, solid Internet resources.

Unlike the broader categories of the first two directories, the Librarians' Index has a front page with a greater variety of topic headings. There are forty-one main headings (it depends a little on how you count — for example, "kids" and "teens" are listed on the same line but are actually two distinct headings). These subdivide into a multitude of subdirectories, which occasionally subdivide again (mostly the subdirectories are headings which lead to actual files— there are usually only a few subdirectories in the list). Over 6,500 sites are listed, all broken down nicely into categories.

Quality of resources is very high, and the whole layout has several unusual and especially valuable characteristics. First, each listing is annotated with a useful summary of the site listed. Details of the annotations are full enough to provide a taste of what you might expect to find, but not so great as to be an overload of information. Second, the author of the annotations and the date of last update are clearly posted, so that you are always fairly confident that what you are viewing has been reviewed recently.

Thirdly, criteria for a site's inclusion in the index are pleasantly rigorous. Several characteristics are necessary for a site to meet the threshold: Content quality (accuracy, factualness, uniqueness, currency, presence of good and stable links, and well-written), Authority (the author's credibility), Scope (vision and intended audience) and Good Design. Commercial sites are discouraged, unless they have

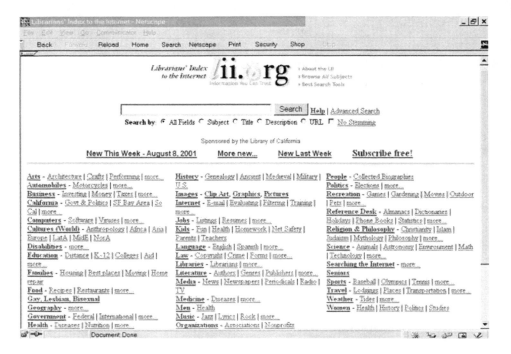

obvious and overwhelming value beyond that of serving as vehicles of merchandising.

The overall result is a compilation of very good Internet resources, well arranged and easy to use. The model is similar to public library systems of classification, and should feel very familiar to anyone who has used an American public library.

THE INTERNET PUBLIC LIBRARY

(http://www.ipl.org/)

This virtual library is an outgrowth of a project from the School of Library and Information Studies at the University of Michigan in 1995. It feels even more like an online public library than the Librarians' Index, and is crammed to bursting with the full-text of a great many works of every description — books of literature and technology, almanacs to handbooks of physics, Sanskrit grammars to online journals. Like most virtual libraries, its coverage is eclectic rather than comprehensive, but the variety of resources is truly impressive.

The IPL arrangement takes a little getting used to, but it is clear enough to navigate your way through from the top page. The collections of the IPL are divided like a public library's into several main sections: Reference, the Reading Room, and an area for Young People.

Reference has several options, including General/Reference, with a standard and comfortable range of almanacs, encyclopedias, dictionaries, etc.; Associations, which lists categories of mostly non-profit organizations; Native Authors, which lists Native American author's works; and Literary Criticism, generally significant works discussing literature.

The Reading Room has likewise four main sections: Texts, Newspapers, Serials and "Other Texts," basically a compilation of texts that do not fit handily in any of the other categories. The first Text category is arranged by Dewey classification, so it is easy enough to browse sections (100's are Philosophy and Religions, 300's Social Sciences, etc.) It contains the largest number of items of any other IPL category, some 15,000 items ranging from selected Mark Twain stories to translations of the early Buddhist work, the Dhammapada.

The only quirk in its arrangement is that the user must know that, like American public libraries, if looking for fiction, you need to search by author or title, as they are not contained in the general grid of Dewey classification. And, like most of the rest of Internet sources, the number and kind of works are limited. Unless the works are in the public domain (written before 1923) U.S. copyright laws usually limit public distribution unless permission has been granted by the author or the author's estate.

The Newspaper section likewise has a bewildering array of newspapers, arranged by region. Range and coverage is very good, as major newspapers invariably have a public website (although some require a free registration, or signup, to use). Massachusetts for example, has over fifty newspapers listed, Argentina over twenty-five, and it is a pleasant diversion to get side-tracked by browsing through their international collection.

The Serials collection is not quite so broad, but still satisfying. Its selection of 3000 plus journals is also, like contemporary texts, limited by the publisher's permission for distribution. This number of serials is likely greater than the number of journals available at all but large city public libraries, but smaller than at a research university. The "Other texts" section defies description, and covers material put out by non-profit organizations like the Victorian Women Writers Project to U.S. Government Publications.

The Internet Public Library is an ongoing project and feels that way. The sheer size of its undertaking guarantees continued development for many years. We can all just be pleased that someone is doing this sort of work.

SPECIALIZED SUBJECT DIRECTORIES

This category covers a bewildering array of resources. Usage of specialized subject directories can be vastly helpful for a number of areas, and one of the difficulties is just the process of discovering what is available for a given interest. There are directories for people (phone directory at http://www.whowhere.lycos.com/Phone) and businesses (Thomas Register of American Manufacturers at http://www.thomasregister.com/), travel (http://www.ricksteves.com/) and jobs (Monster.com at http://monster.com/), colleges and universities (Peterson's Guide at http://www.petersons.com/).

The sheer range and depth of coverage of these specialized directories is astonishing. For more information on selected subject area directories, as well as other Internet resources, see the page linked to the book *Internet Research*, at http://userwww.sfsu.edu/~fielden/internetresearch.htm#subjects.

6

Future of Search Engines

The real problem is not whether machines think,
but whether men do. — B.F. Skinner

What can we expect from the search engine designers in the next decade? What directions are search engines likely to develop? Will we recognize search engines in 20 years as anything resembling our current applications?

The Web is still an infant, although one that has grown so far and so fast it is sometimes hard to remember its recent birth. It is also a five hundred pound baby, and generally grows where it wants, whether people like it or not.

The whole process of research, the seeking of answers to questions posed, could do with considerably more study. The online world introduces some quirks into the research process, and cognitive scientists and psychologists, along with members of the Information Retrieval field, will do well to unravel more fully the kinds of paths and decisions individuals take when conducting research.

What are the problem areas? Spam and commercial pressures will continue to disrupt the best search engine operation. Perhaps some regulation will take place, or standards developed (and adopted) that make for improved sorting and classifying documents. Web documents may develop different formats that work better for indexing.

What languages will be represented in search engine design? English is already a dominant force on the Internet; will it become more so over time? How will search engines deal with increasing numbers of documents with non–Latin scripts such as Devanagri or Arabic? AltaVista began the trend of automated translation, but this is such a complicated task that all kinds of room for development is present.

Will search engines become credible mind-readers? This is only a half-joking question. Will your browser become the archive and repository of your tendencies, your wants and special needs?

Where are humans in all of this? Will a new generation of Internet librarians emerge to serve the world? Or will the human help come in other forms, with better directories and patterns of Web subject cataloging?

IMPROVED DOCUMENT STANDARDS

One of the difficulties of any new technology is the challenge of making and adopting standards: of vocabulary, acceptable practices, methods of communication, and of the general welfare for all.

One of the major problems for search engines right now is preparing indexes for the documents. So many documents are currently in a format that is barely standardized. The most basic Web documents only need the barest minimum of "tags" that identify them as such and enable them to be read by a browser. Not even a document title, author or date of creation are required, and plenty of documents that are missing all or some of those normally expected features are present out on the Web.

Some attempts at increasing the level of document standards have been made, and the Dublin Core initiative* is one such movement. Increased use of these kinds of standards will assist search engines in their attempt to index the Web.

In the near future several features already in place will likely evolve further. Spelling checks such as employed by AltaVista and Google will become more prevalent and help rule out a major problem

*http://dublincore.org/documents/dces/ [Oct. 2001].

with many searches. More work may be done with stemming algorithms to match a greater range of related keywords. This sort of "fuzzy logic" should be promising, and as more experience is gathered, the results may improve as well.

TERM MAPPING

The step first taken by Excite has several interesting implications. If keywords can be mapped to concept terms, two normally contradictory aspects of Information Retrieval may be brought closer together, and results will be both more precise and have greater recall. The means to do this will involve the use of a specially constructed thesaurus, which can make connections between keywords entered and a standardized list of concept terms. This method will be one way to combine the best of both worlds, by utilizing human ingenuity for the concept thesaurus, but employing the speed and range of computers in actually doing the mapping during a search.

The kinds of people most likely to provide some interesting insights into this process will be those engaged in linguistics, along with those who know the potential user base the best and also something about how people go about searching: the librarians and cognitive scientists who study this complicated process.

NON-BOOLEAN SYSTEMS

Boolean systems will gradually become less and less prevalent, perhaps disappearing altogether. A variety of more flexible query systems, represented today by vector space and probabilistic systems, will become more adept at matching user queries with documents. The mathematics will take advantage of newer applied models, using neural network and other experimental frameworks.

Probably some work will occur in "smart" systems, that learn from queries posed. These expert systems will be able to customize themselves to a user's profile, and make simple judgments about the probabilities of a given document matching a user's desire.

Expert "Smart" Systems

This is an area long overdue for greater attention. Relevance feedback depends on decisions made by the searcher, after an initial search is run, to modify or redirect searches already made into new and more promising directions. If it were possible to take advantage of various tendencies exhibited by the individual searcher over time (by collecting search histories of previous searches, having searches work within a customized filter or profile the searcher generated) then search results could potentially be much improved.

Already the commercial world has been adept at this kind of activity, and marketers have known for generations how to tap into their potential clients' interests and idiosyncrasies in ways that will attract their attention.

One of the difficulties of this approach is that there is a need to allow the user the freedom to tailor the system. Currently many experienced searchers would be unlikely to shift decision-making behaviors over to a machine and would prefer the greatest amount of control over the customizing. New searchers might be more willing to let the machine do more of the calculating.

Some data on this piece of the puzzle may lie in statistics about the search engines' users who prefer "expert" or "advanced" search interfaces. What do these more experienced searchers do with their more powerful choices at this level? How could these advantages be extended?

Non–Text Format Indexing

We have briefly mentioned some of the difficulties of indexing the world of non-text documents. These include the problems posed by document titling practices, the fact that images do not lend themselves to self-derived indexing data the way text documents do, and generally poor attention to "index friendly" information accompanying the image, audio file or video. This is another arena where lack of standardization impoverishes the whole collection and creates hurdles to good access.

It is not the case that specialists do not recognize the importance of standard ways of handling non-text files such as images. Standards are handy but tend to be adopted only by narrow special-interest groups: e.g. architects, or botanists handling image databases of specimens. Coming up with a set of standards to be used by everyone connected with a particular non-text format will be a formidable challenge.

Until the formats begin to include some sort of metadata themselves, beginning with such information as author, date of creation, perhaps place of creation, and so on, and have this embedded in the document itself, non–text document indexing will be very problematic, and no amount of computing power will prove very productive.

VISUAL NAVIGATION

The Web has done very well with the advent of the browsers' graphic user interface, and there is no reason not to think that this spatial model will prove useful for organizing documents, making it easier for people to visualize where documents are, and how related documents might be represented as "neighbors." Documents with many facets can be listed a number of different ways, and filters might be customizable to turn off and on as a particular facet is needed. The vector space model itself is a three-dimensional environment, and experimenting with this extra dimension in document space may prove very helpful.

The trouble with the vector space model is that it is not in fact a true representation of "document space," but a superimposed construct. Whether some cataloging scheme can actually become adept at locating documents this way remains to be seen, but surely shows some promise as one measure of displaying document likeness.

Coming up with the "killer application" in the search engine competition would be a feather in any company's cap, but will companies in the business of information retrieval be able to ignore the large profits available with advertising or other still-to-be-dreamed up marketing plans? Who will the search engine companies be hiring to do this work? Will there only be computer science folks, or will more research and development be done in theoretical areas such as cognitive science or computational linguistics? Will the librarian's ethos of advocate for the user become a greater part of the picture? And as automated functions proliferate, is there any danger that they will diverge from the intentions of their creators? Will users know or care about these developments?

When search engines and directories first arrived on the Internet scene in the mid-1990s there was a great deal of hope that they would solve a myriad of information location troubles. While they have undoubtedly been a boon, a great deal of development is still required. The gap between what humans want from their computer tools and what the tools are capable of delivering is still great.

Luckily, this arena has captured the interest of some very keen minds, and unless the rush and obsession with profit ruins everything, we can expect a good future for better methods of finding information. Hopefully, this progress will outstrip our apparent desire to populate the universe with ever more and lengthier records of our existence — our documents, images, and ephemera of every description. It is our job as intelligent humans to turn our information into knowledge, and to become wiser stewards of our collective civilization.

Glossary

Algorithm A mathematical formula that allows certain computer functions to operate. Search engines use these formulas to calculate relevance and rank retrieval sets.

Boolean system A mechanism employing set logic for searching databases. for arranging sets of records. Employs the three standard Boolean operators AND, OR and NOT (sometimes AND NOT) to combine keywords into a query that the database can process.

Bots see crawlers

Client A client program runs on your machine and asks for information from a "server" that dishes up the requested documents. A Web browser is a client, which can contact Web servers for their documents.

Crawlers also bots, spiders, etc. Automated programs employed by the search engines to locate URLs and make index entries for their content and potential retrieval.

Directory Also referred to as an Internet index. A hierarchical arrangement of URLs ordered by topic, usually accomplished by human indexers.

Document Used in its broadest and most basic form, a document is any item of information, which may be a manuscript, webpage, spreadsheet file, image, movie clip or audio file. When speaking of document retrieval, we mean the location and access of the item in question. Search Engines can look for all different kinds of documents.

Extended Boolean   A Boolean system with enhancements (fuzzy logic, weighted words).

Graphical User Interface (GUI)   A computer interface that allows the use of graphics for navigation. Pioneered by the Macintosh computer operating system, these usually take advantage of a mouse's point-and-click capacity. Web browsers like Netscape Navigator and Microsoft's Internet Explorer are examples of GUI browsers.

Human Computer Interaction   Field of study that examines the relationship and communication between computers and humans. HCI attempts to smooth and simplify communication whenever possible, and to create "intuitive" computer mediated tools that are easy and understandable.

Hyperlinks   Also "links." The basis for the World Wide Web, hyperlinks are text in a document that "point" to another file or location, which then can be reached by a mouse-click on the hyperlinked text.

Index   A tool for finding and locating information. In its simplest form, an index is a list that pairs a topic with a location. Internet indexes are often called directories, and are lists of Internet resources with their listed URLs.

Information Literacy   A developed ability to find, analyze, process and communicate information. Combines the elements of computer literacy (proficiency with computer tools) with critical thinking. An important element of research methods for most disciplines.

Information Retrieval   Field of study which focuses on the location of documents, using various mathematical models to define "alikeness" of various documents.

Interface   The "communication zone" between human and computer. A search engine has an interface that consists of a query window, various buttons and navigational devices that allow a user to pose a query to the database.

Invisible Web   That part of the World Wide Web outside the range of search engine crawlers. Includes pages that require a password or registration, proprietary databases available only by subscription, Intranets, pages with no links pointing at them, and pages deliberately excluded from crawler visits.

Keywords   The basis of a query, keywords are the most essential terms that describe a given topic. Keywords form the basis by which the search engine finds matches among its list of documents.

Metadata   Information about a document, usually includes author, title, subject description, format, etc.

Metatags   The HTML tags hidden from normal view that describe the page's content, author, date of creation — the metadata — or information about the document.

Natural language processing   The ability of a search engine to handle a query that is more like what someone would say if they were talking to another human. "What is the capital of Libya?" is a natural language query, rather than a Boolean "capital AND libya."

Phrases   Combination of words that exist in a specified order and distance (must make an exact match).

Portal   A large, multi-faceted Internet site offering a wide arrange of Internet services: often mail, chat-groups, shopping services, etc.

Precision   A measure of information retrieval. Any given query will deliver results, which can be described as having high recall (large numbers) or high precision (high degree of relevancy). Recall and precision are usually inversely related — high recall usually means low precision and vice versa.

Probabilistic   A non–Boolean system of ranking a query result set, whereby results are ordered in decreasing rank of relevancy. It is characterized by term weighting and good potential for relevance feedback.

Query   A word or combination of words typed into a window of a search engine which is then matched against the search engine's database of index entries.

Recall   see precision.

Relevance feedback A mechanism built into a search engine that permits modification or rephrasing of an initial query, depending on the decisions and input from the user.

Search engine Any of a category of Internet finding tools that use an automated index to build a searchable database of websites. The user types the desired search keywords into a search box, and the search engine retrieves a set of records that match the terms, putting them into an order that is deemed useful for the searcher to browse.

Server Computer that accepts requests for information and delivers files from its storage. A Web server delivers webpages when they are requested by a person or a crawler.

Spam Originally junk email, unwanted advertising that appeared in your mail box. Expanded definition includes webpages whose advertising intent leads them to try to deceive search engines' indexes and push their placement as high as possible for a given query set.

Spiders See crawlers.

Stopwords Non-important words that a search engine will discard in a search. Common stopwords in English include articles ("a," "an," and "the") plus most prepositions ("with," "for," "about" etc).

Syntax The rules that govern how search terms are combined. In Boolean systems, terms must be combined according to set rules.

Truncation Also "stemming," which means a search for the root of the word in its multiple spin-off variations. Usually accomplished by a non-alphabetic character (often an asterisk) the search term farm* will deliver farm, farmers, farming, farm-machinery, etc.

URL Uniform Resource Locator. The Web "address" of a given document. Web documents are conventionally written with a prefix "http://" which stands for "hypertext transfer protocol," then gives the words that map to an actual numerical (IP) address. Often URLs are given without the understood prefix, so we can say for this book's page to go to www.library.sfsu.edu/fielden/seh.htm

Vector space   An information retrieval system that makes use of a "document space" for clustering similar documents. The degree of similarity is computed by means of calculating vectors of various document elements.

Selected Bibliography

Ackermann, E. C., and K. Hartman. *Searching and Researching on the Internet and the World Wide Web.* Wilsonville, OR: Franklin Beedle, 1998.

Belew, Richard K. *Finding Out About: A Cognitive Perspective on Search Engine Technology and the WWW.* Cambridge, U.K.: Cambridge University Press, 2000.

Berry, Michael W. *Understanding Search Engines: Mathematical Modeling and Text Retrieval.* Philadelphia, PA: Society for Industrial and Applied Mathematics, 1999.

Glossbrenner, Alfred. *Search Engines for the World Wide Web.* Berkeley, CA: Peachpit Press, 1999.

Hock, Randolph. *The Extreme Searcher's Guide to Web Search Engines: A Handbook for the Serious Searcher.* Medford, NJ: CyberAge Books, 2001.

Introna, L., and H. Nissenbaum. "Defining the Web: The Politics of Search Engines." *Computer* 33 (2000).

Maze, Susan. *Authoritative Guide to Web Search Engines.* New York: Neal-Schuman, 1997.

Notess, Greg. "Search Engine Showdown: The Users' Guide to Web Searching." [http://www.searchengineshowdown.com].

Sullivan, Danny. "Search Engine Watch." [http://searchenginewatch.com].

Index

Terms in *italics* appear in the Glossary. **Bold** numbers indicate pages that have a more central focus when multiple entries exist.